# FAIRY TALE PRINCESS COLORING BOOK:

## ENCHANTED REALMS

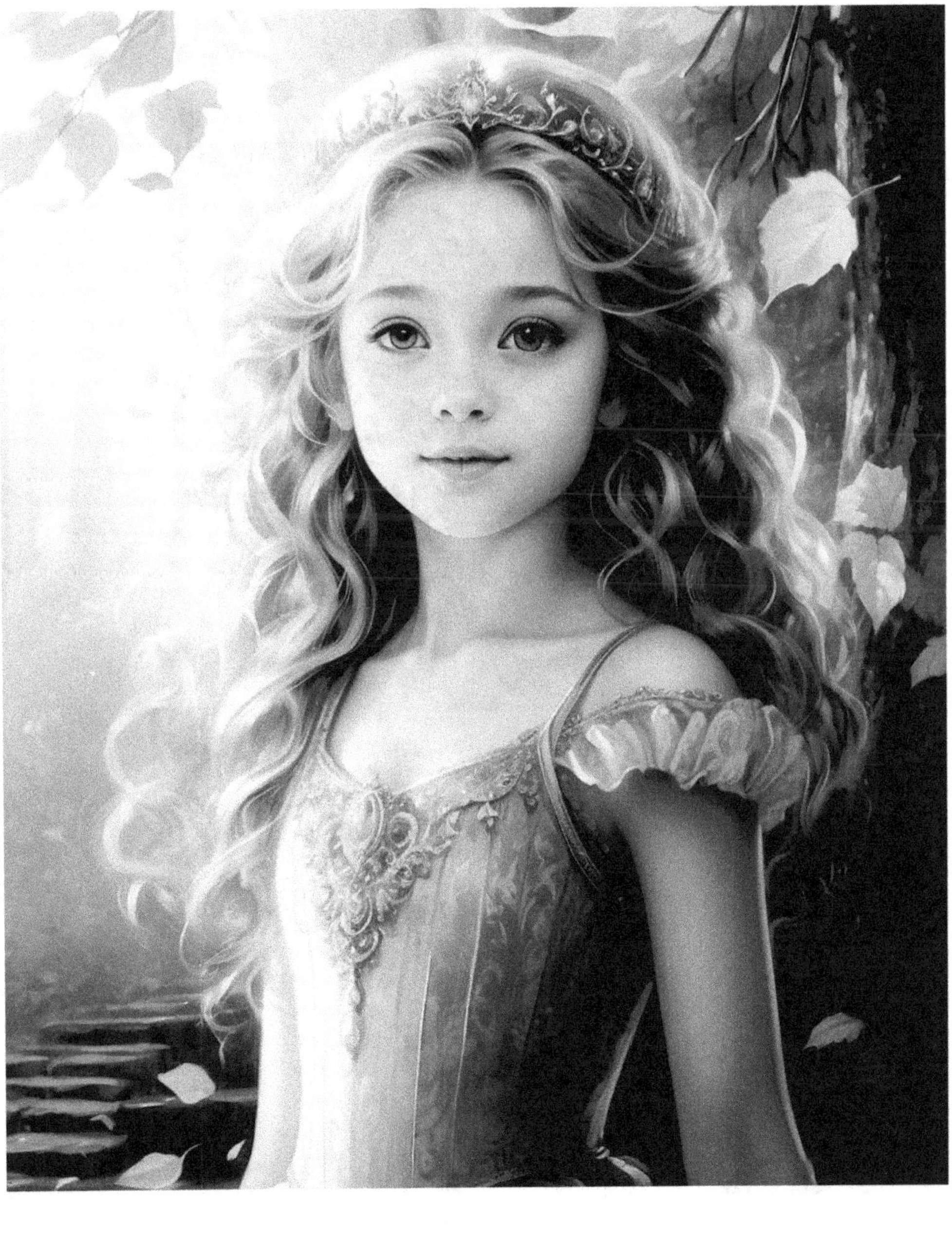

Join our Creativity Circle:
Scan the QR code to subscribe for free
coloring books and stay updated on our
latest releases.
Follow us on social media for additional
inspiration and exclusive content.
Be part of our creative community today.

SCAN ME

 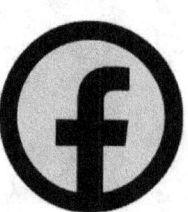 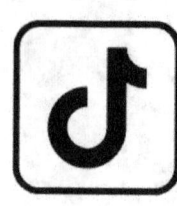

# Thank You

### and

Welcome to "Fairy Tale Princess Coloring Book: Enchanted Realms, Sakurer

As you open the pages of "Fairy Tale Princess Coloring Books: Enchanted Realms," we at SCC want to extend a heartfelt thank you, Sakurer, for embarking on this magical journey with us. This book is a gateway into a world where fairy tale enchantment and artistry blend seamlessly.

Each illustration has been crafted with care and attention to detail, inviting you to explore the nuances of greyscale art and the timeless beauty of fairy tales. These pages are not just illustrations; they are stories waiting to be told through your unique artistic lens.

As a valued member of our creative community, your touch transforms each page from a mere sketch to a vibrant tale of fantasy and wonder. Your participation enriches the SCC legacy, celebrating our shared love for art and storytelling.

We eagerly await to see how your creativity will bring these fairy tale princesses and their realms to life.

Happy coloring, Sakurer, and thank you for being an integral part of this enchanting journey.

Sakura
Creativity Circle

# TEST YOUR COLORS HERE

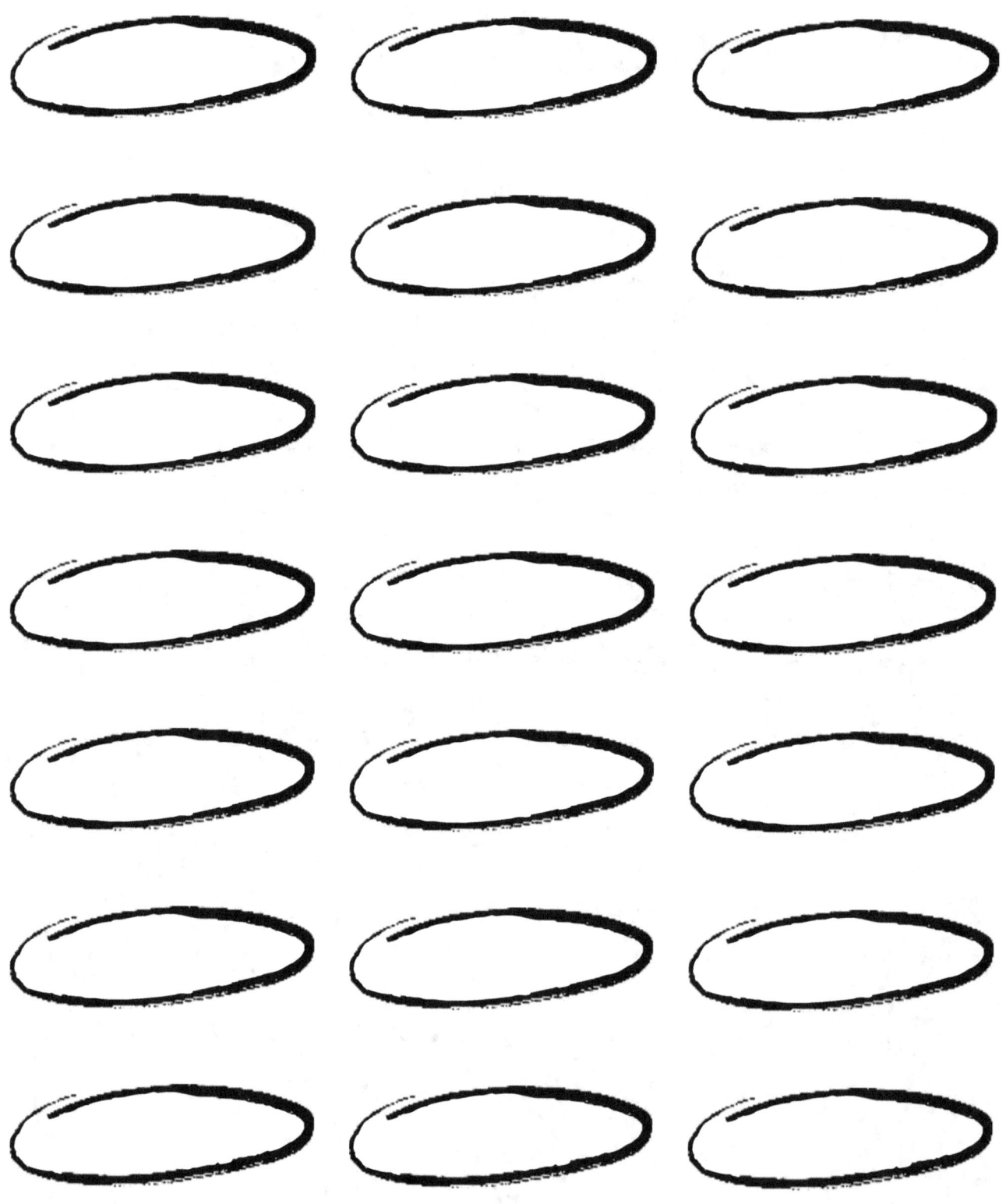

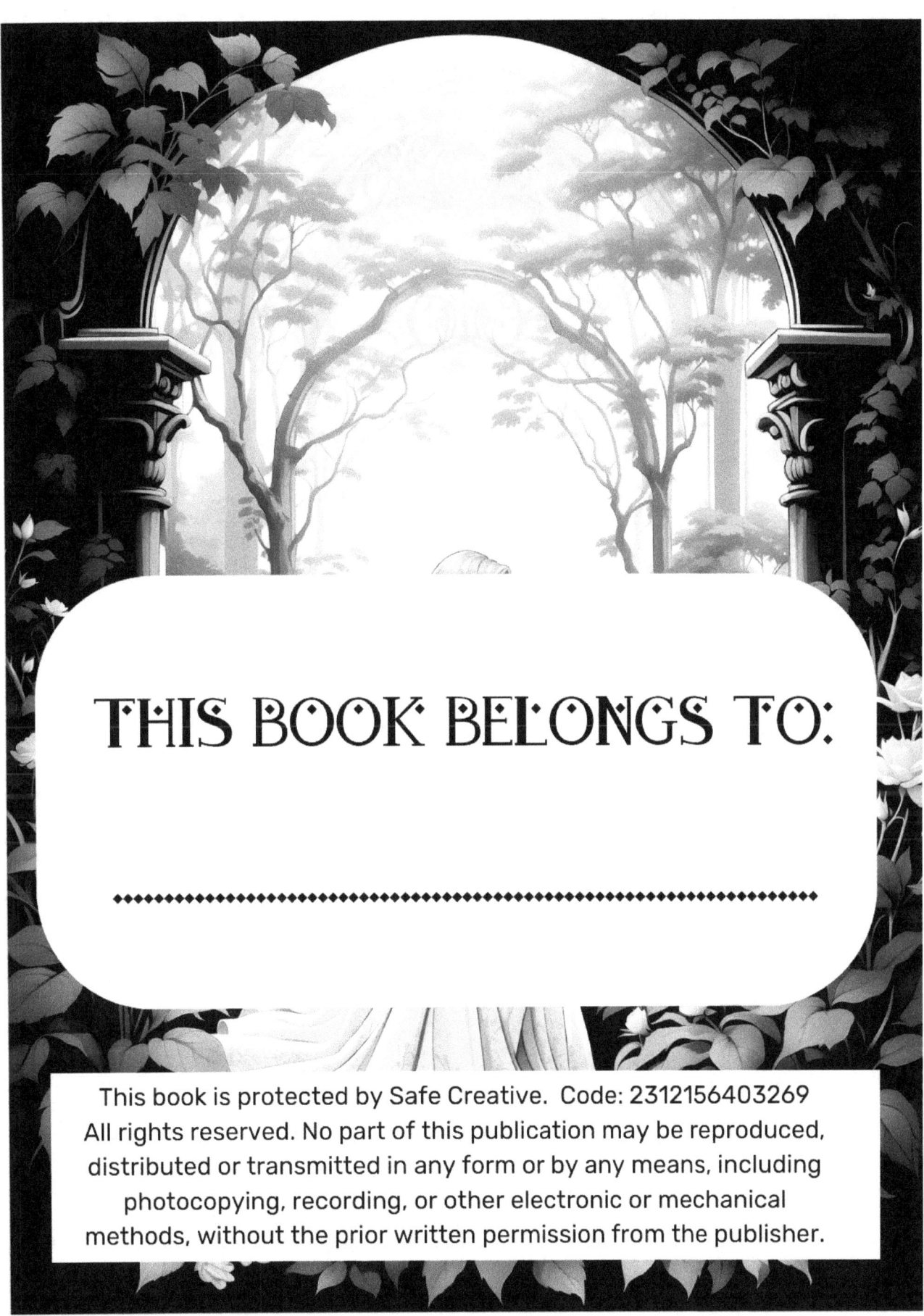

# THIS BOOK BELONGS TO:

◆◆◆◆◆◆◆◆◆◆◆◆◆◆◆◆◆◆◆◆◆◆◆◆◆◆◆◆◆◆◆◆◆◆◆◆◆◆◆◆◆◆◆◆◆◆◆◆◆◆◆

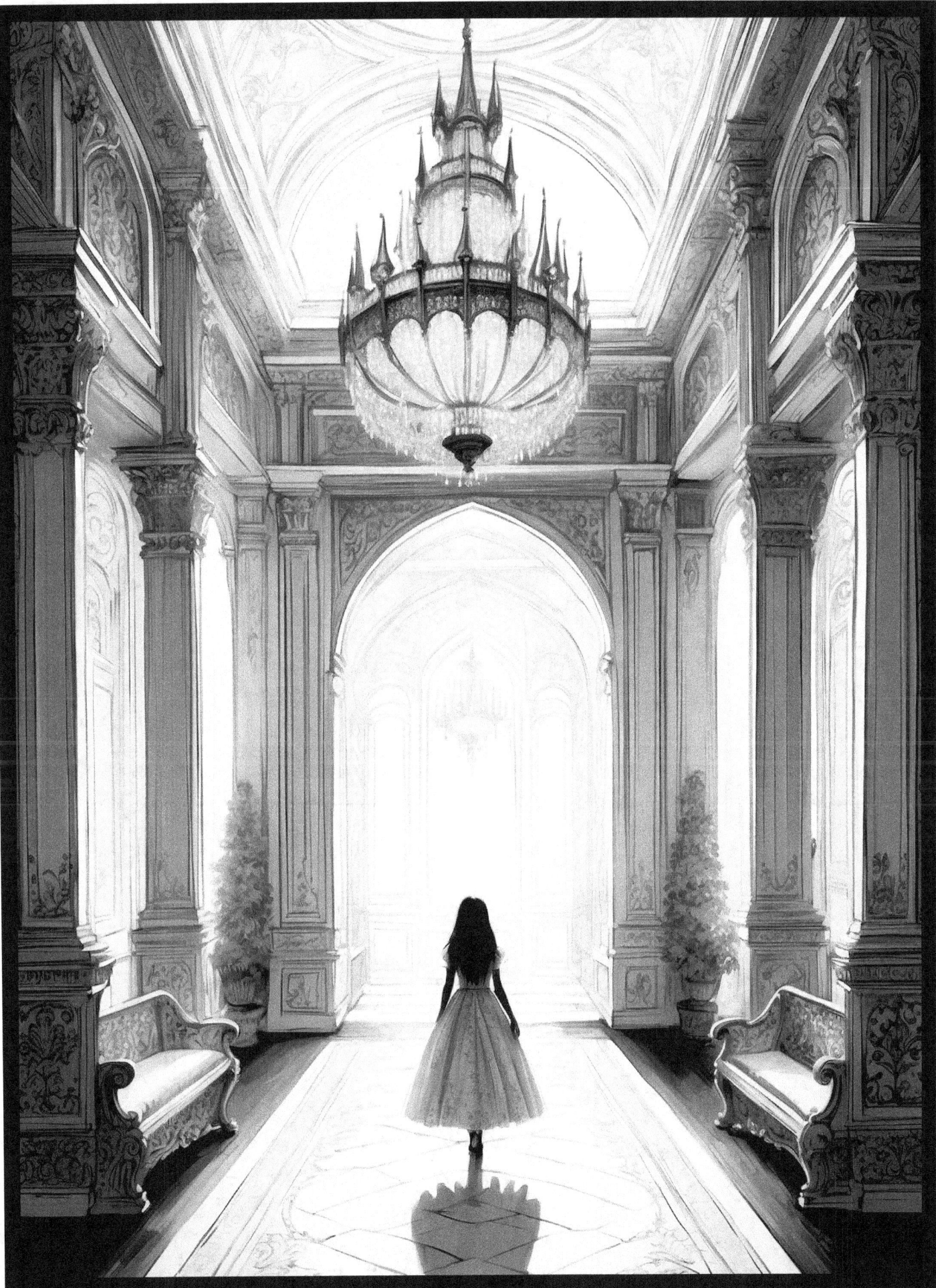

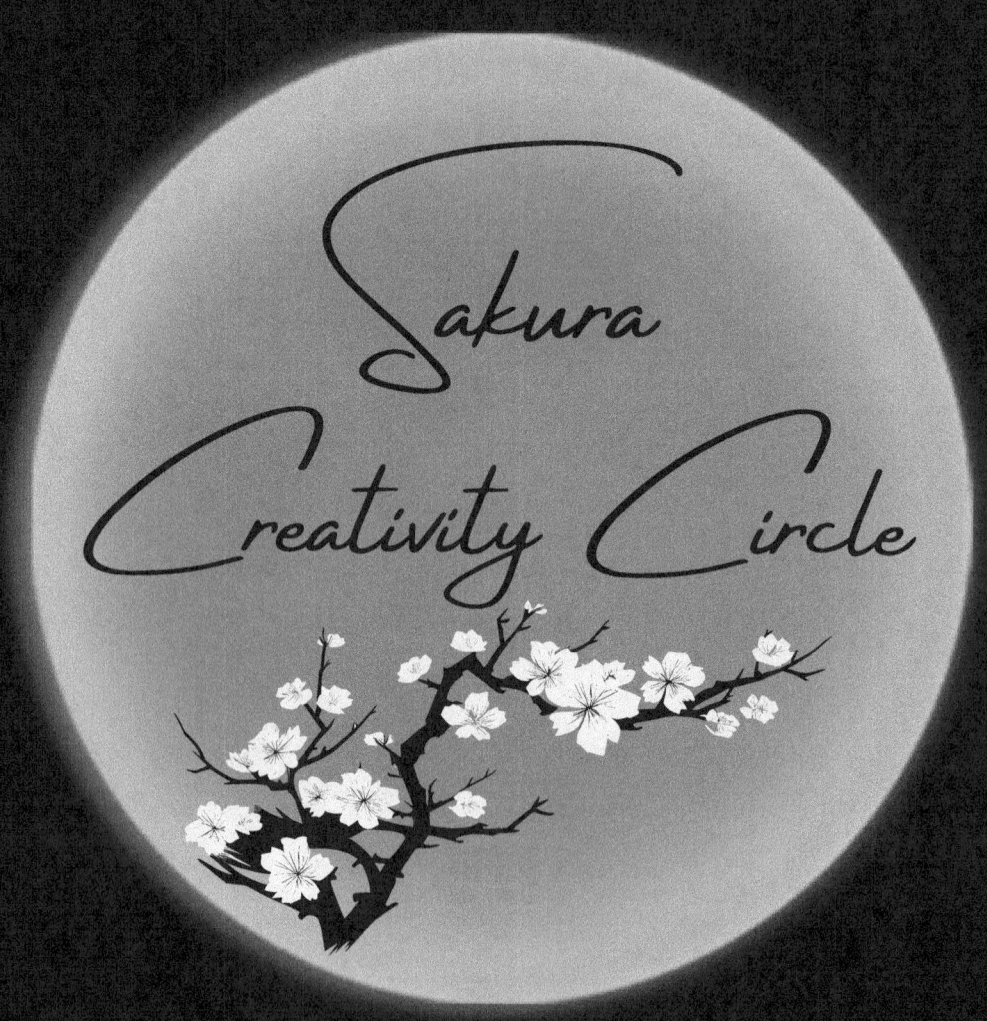

sakuracreativitycircle.com

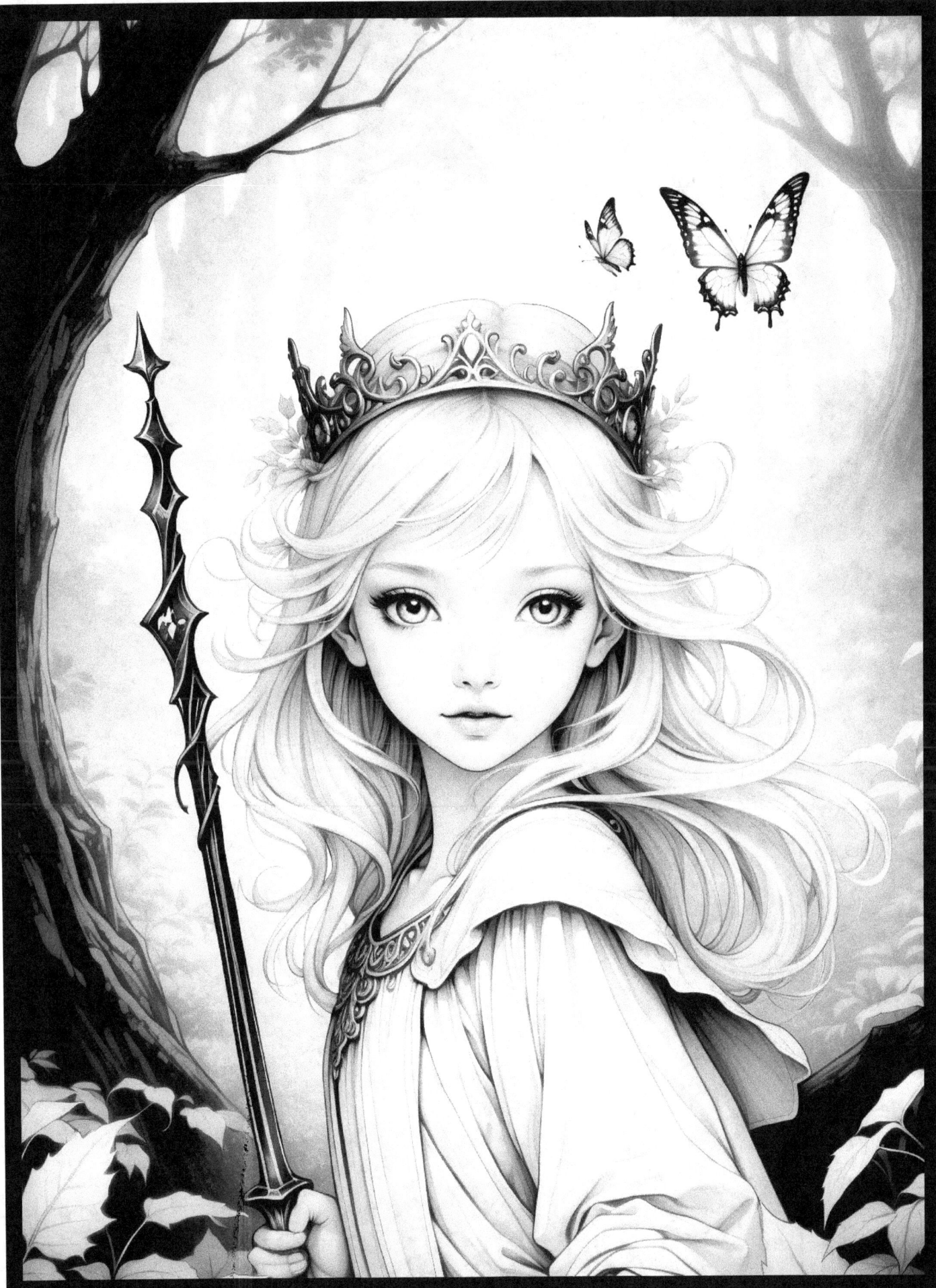

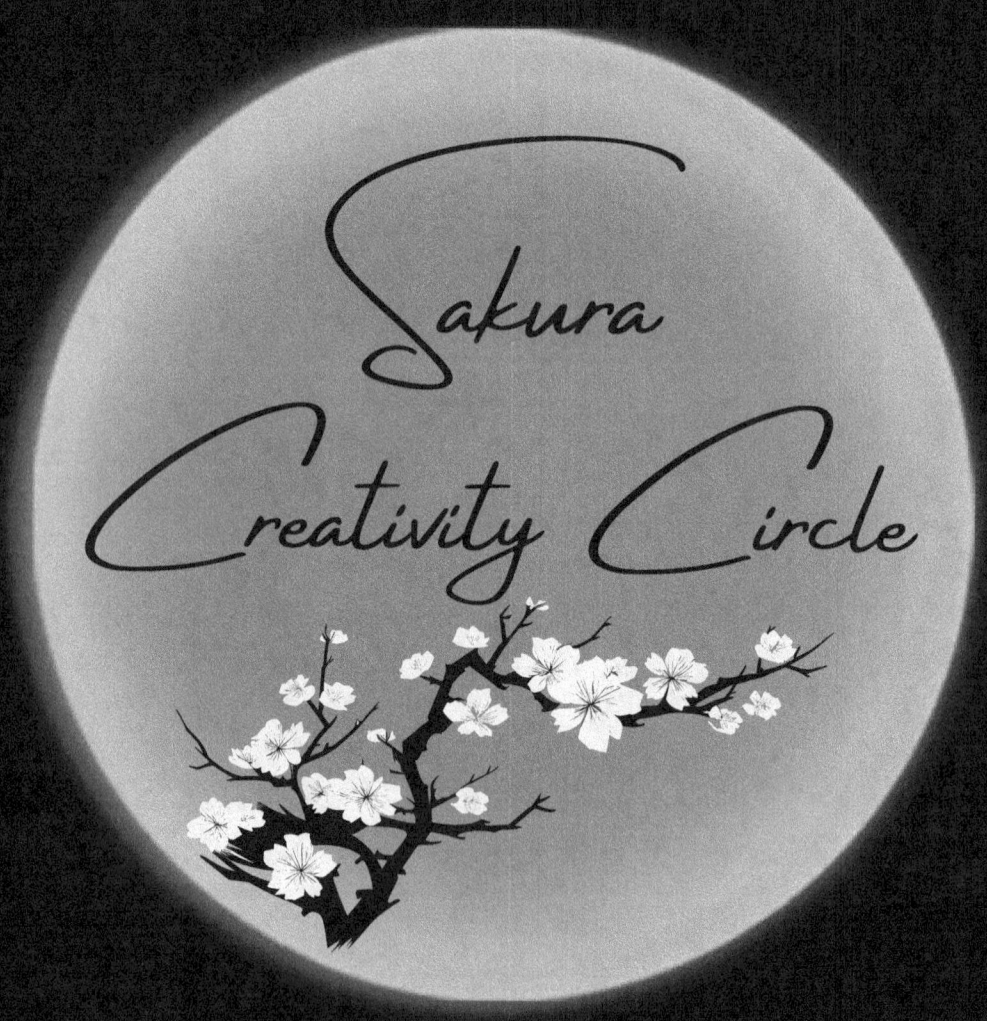

sakuracreativitycircle.com

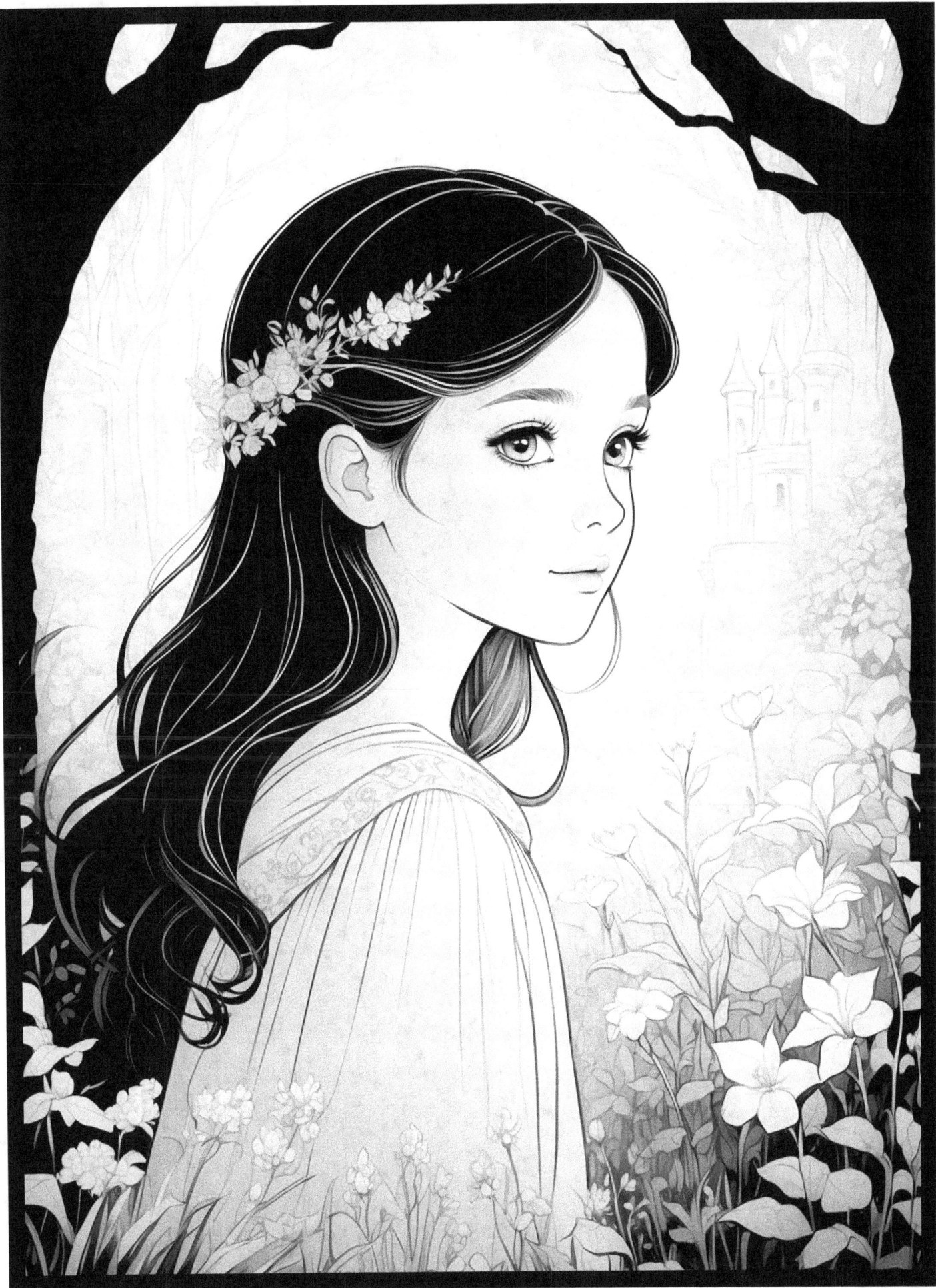

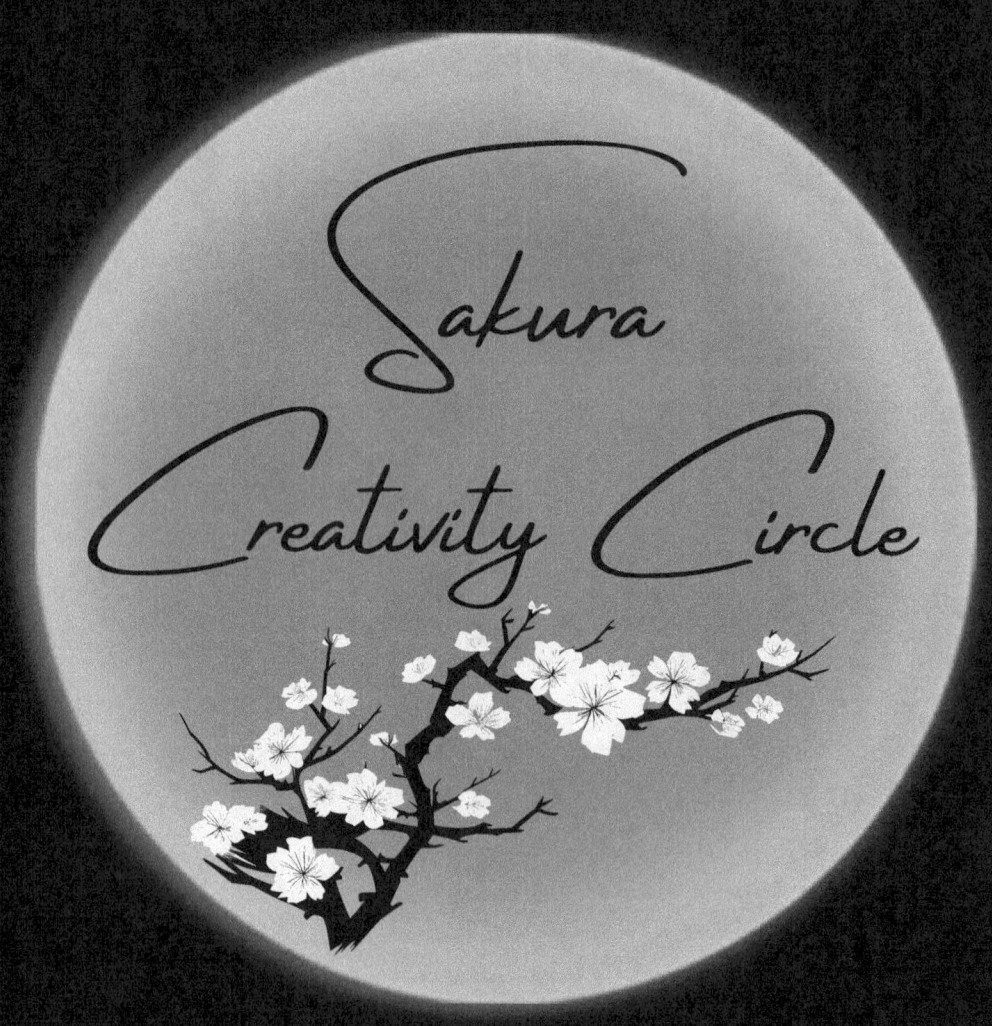

sakuracreativitycircle.com

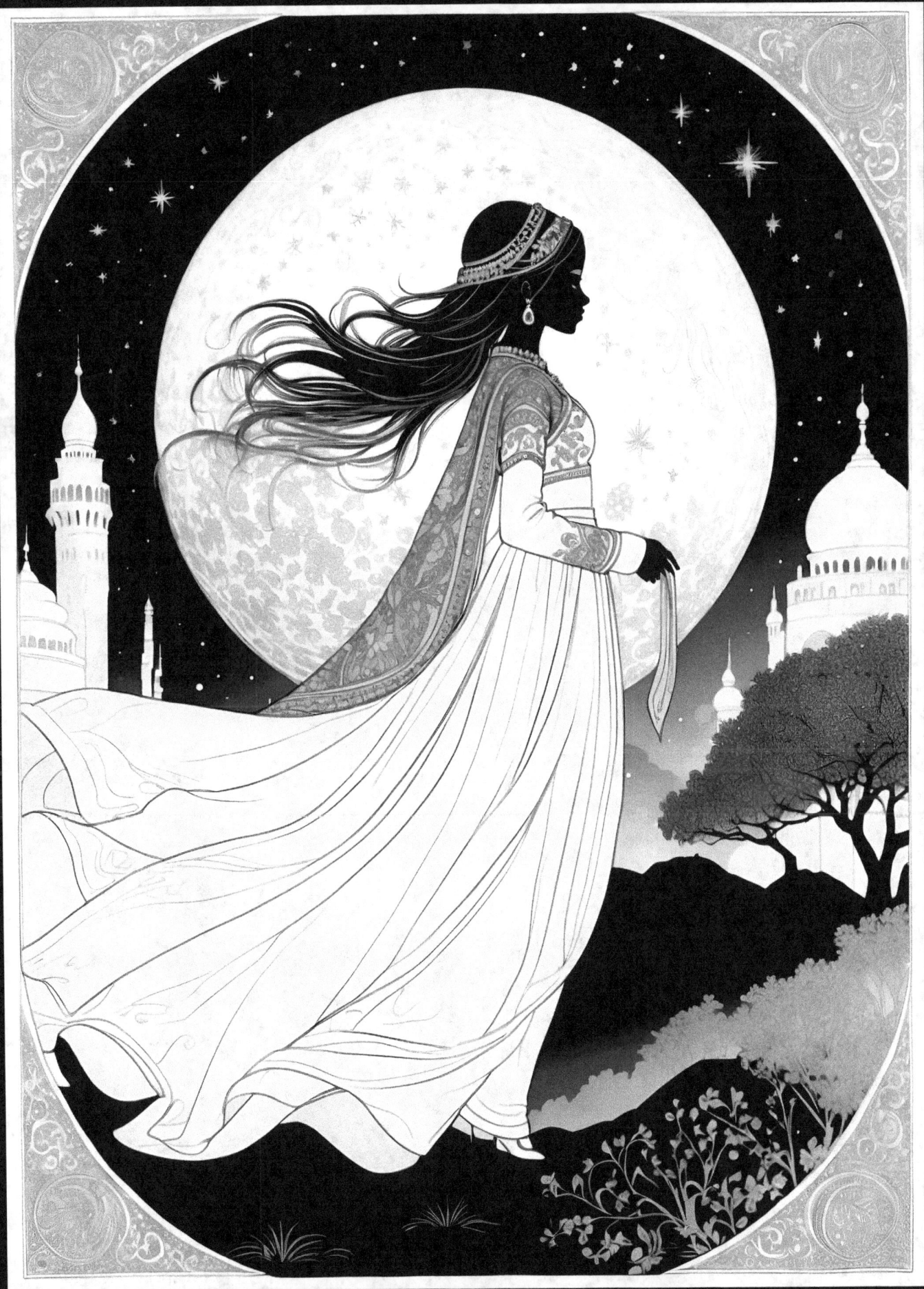

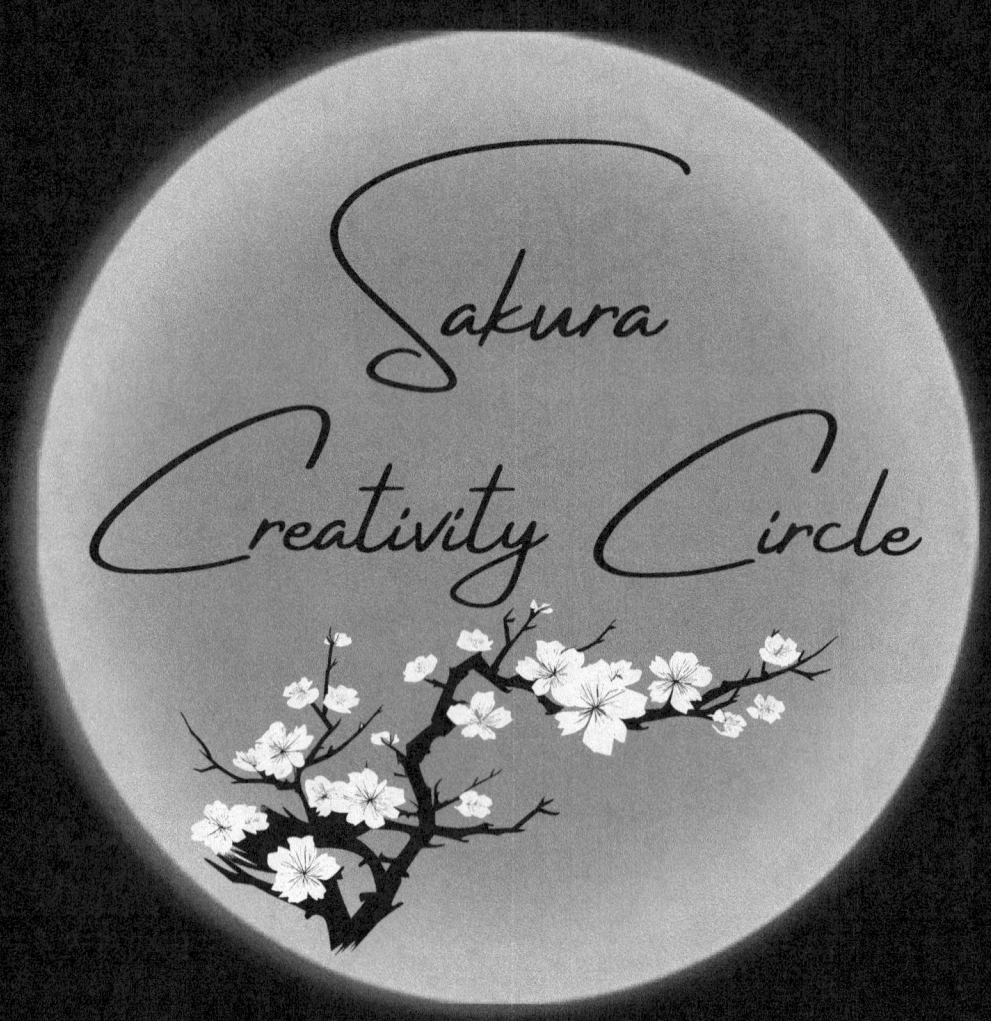

sakuracreativitycircle.com

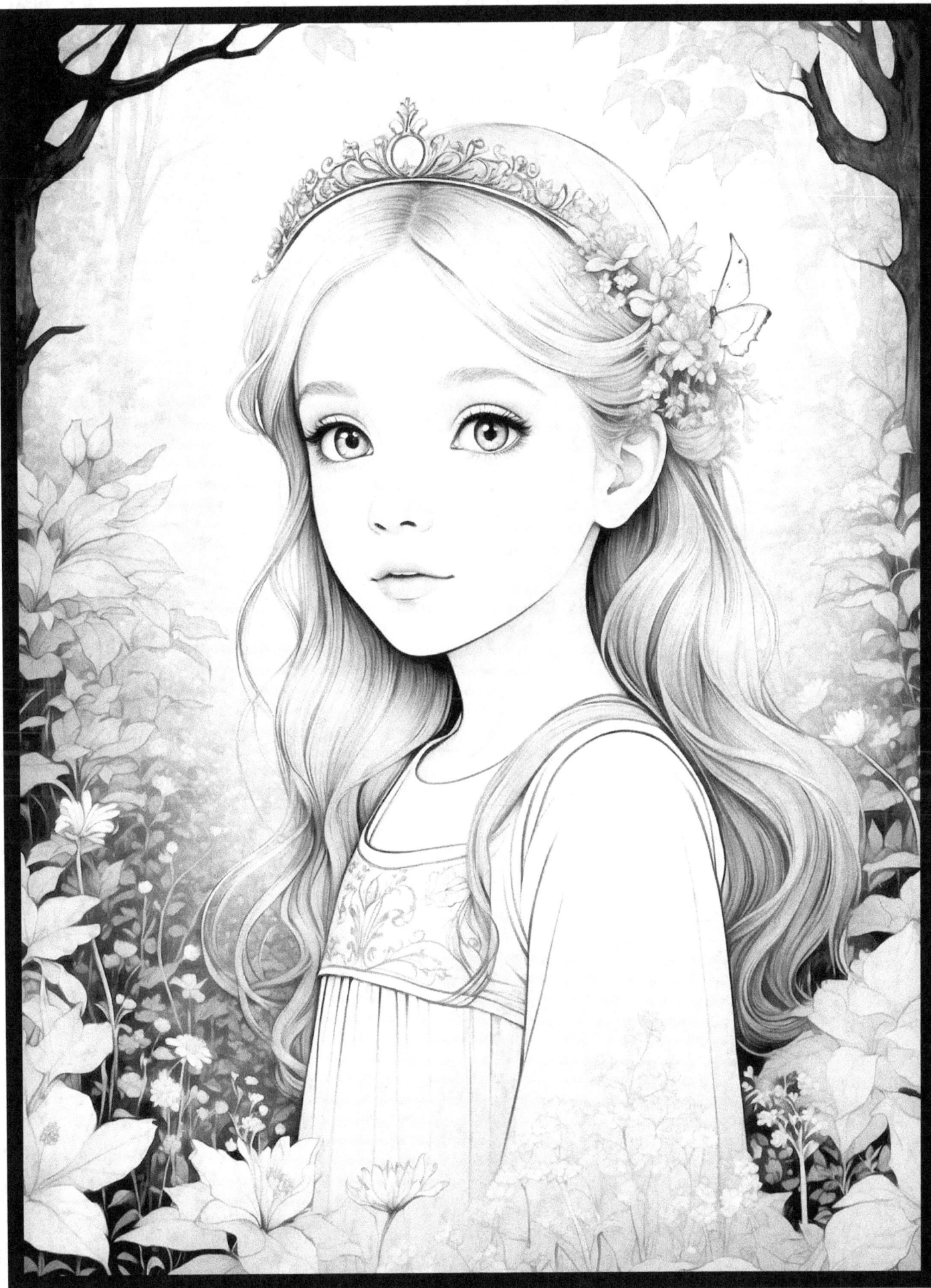

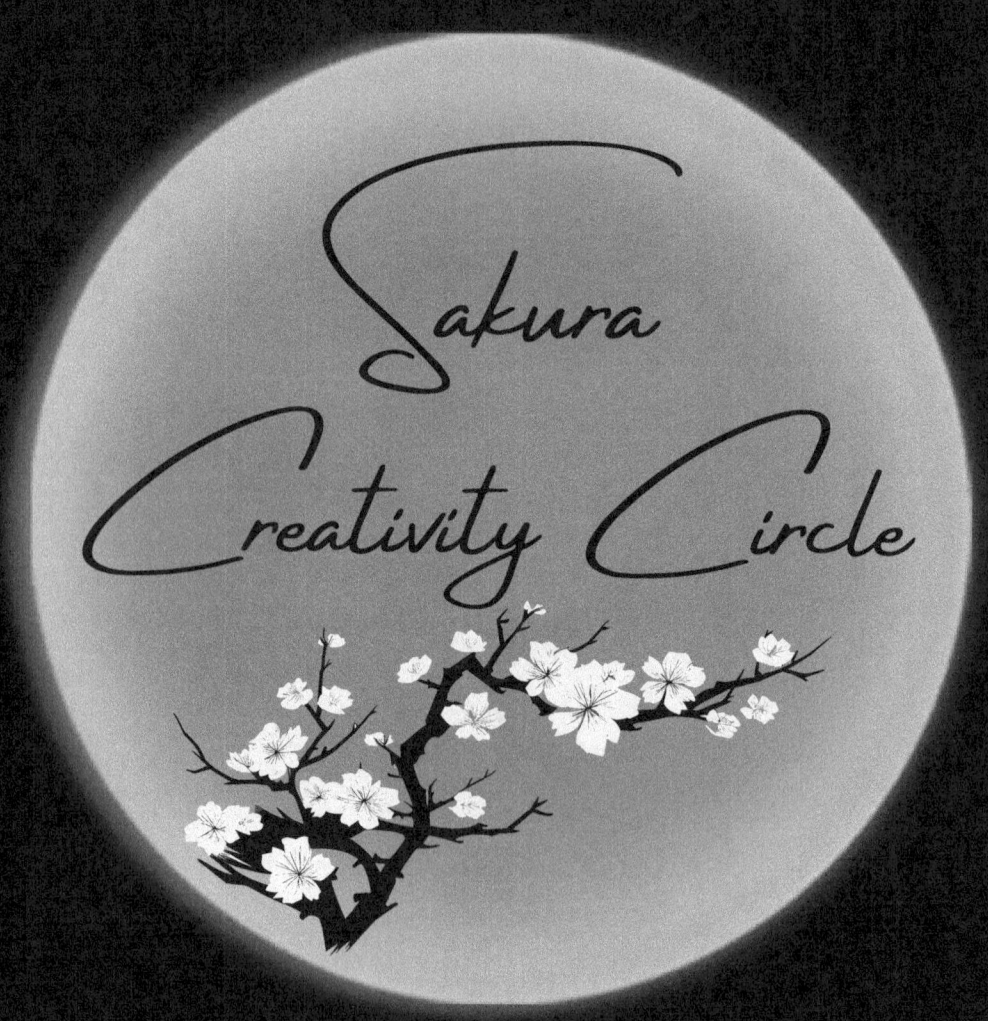

sakuracreativitycircle.com

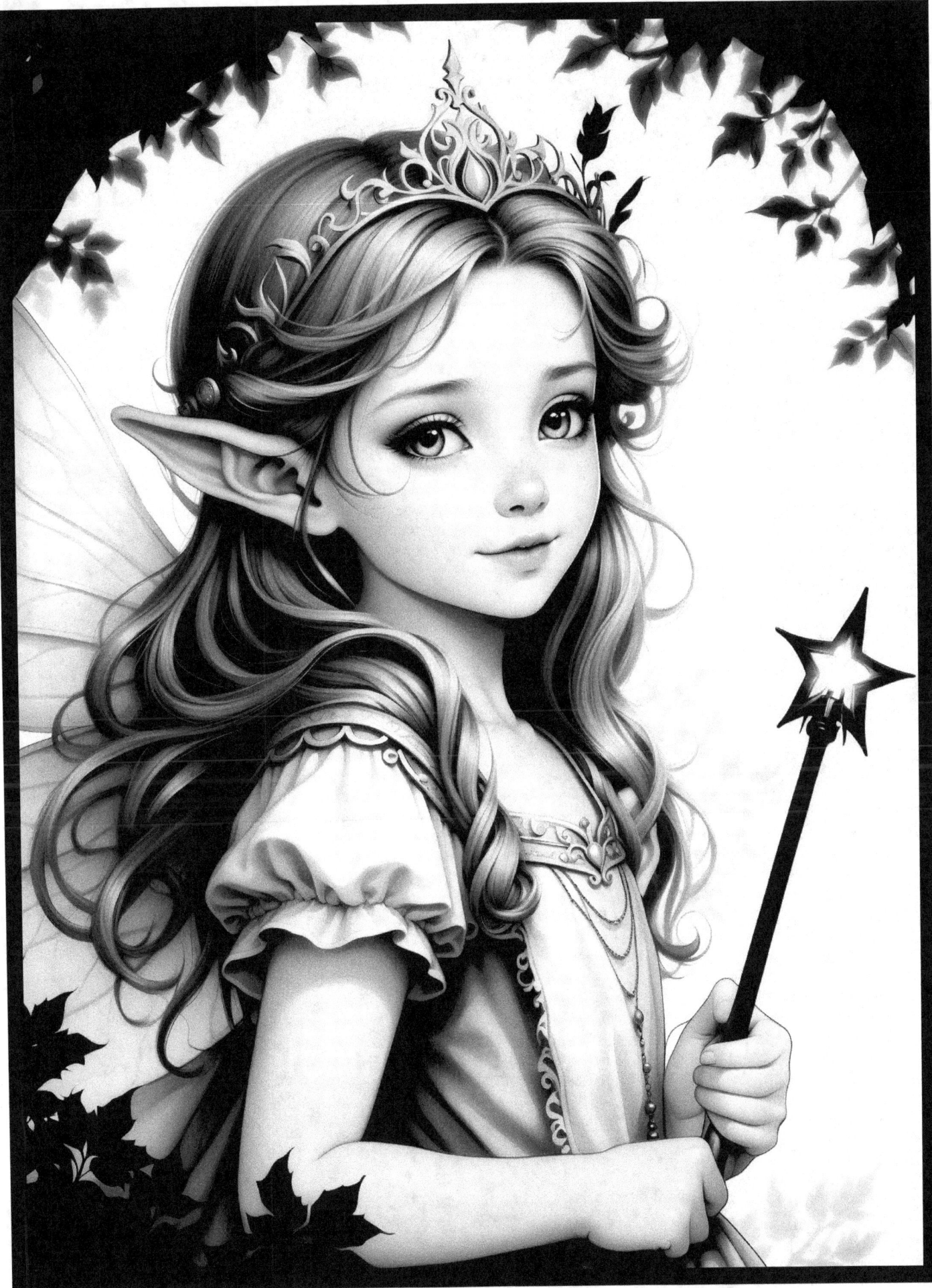

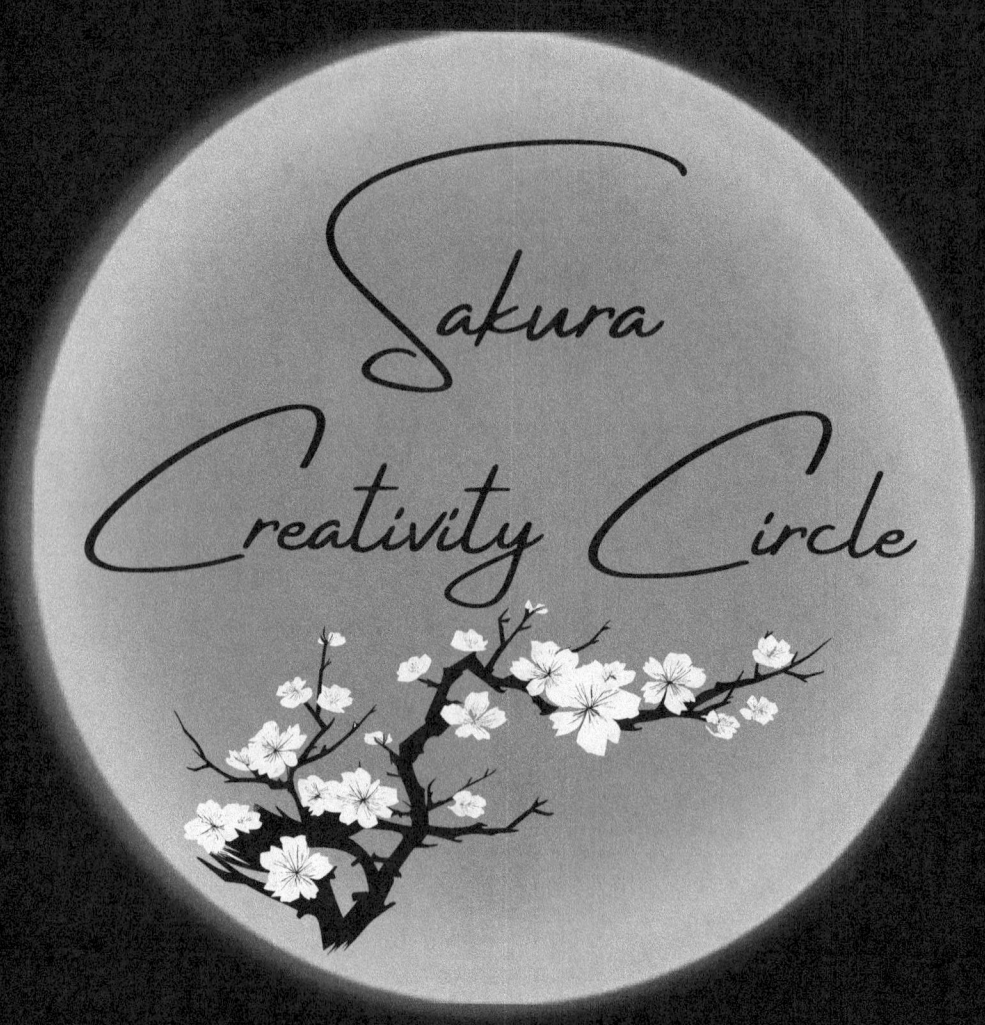

sakuracreativitycircle.com

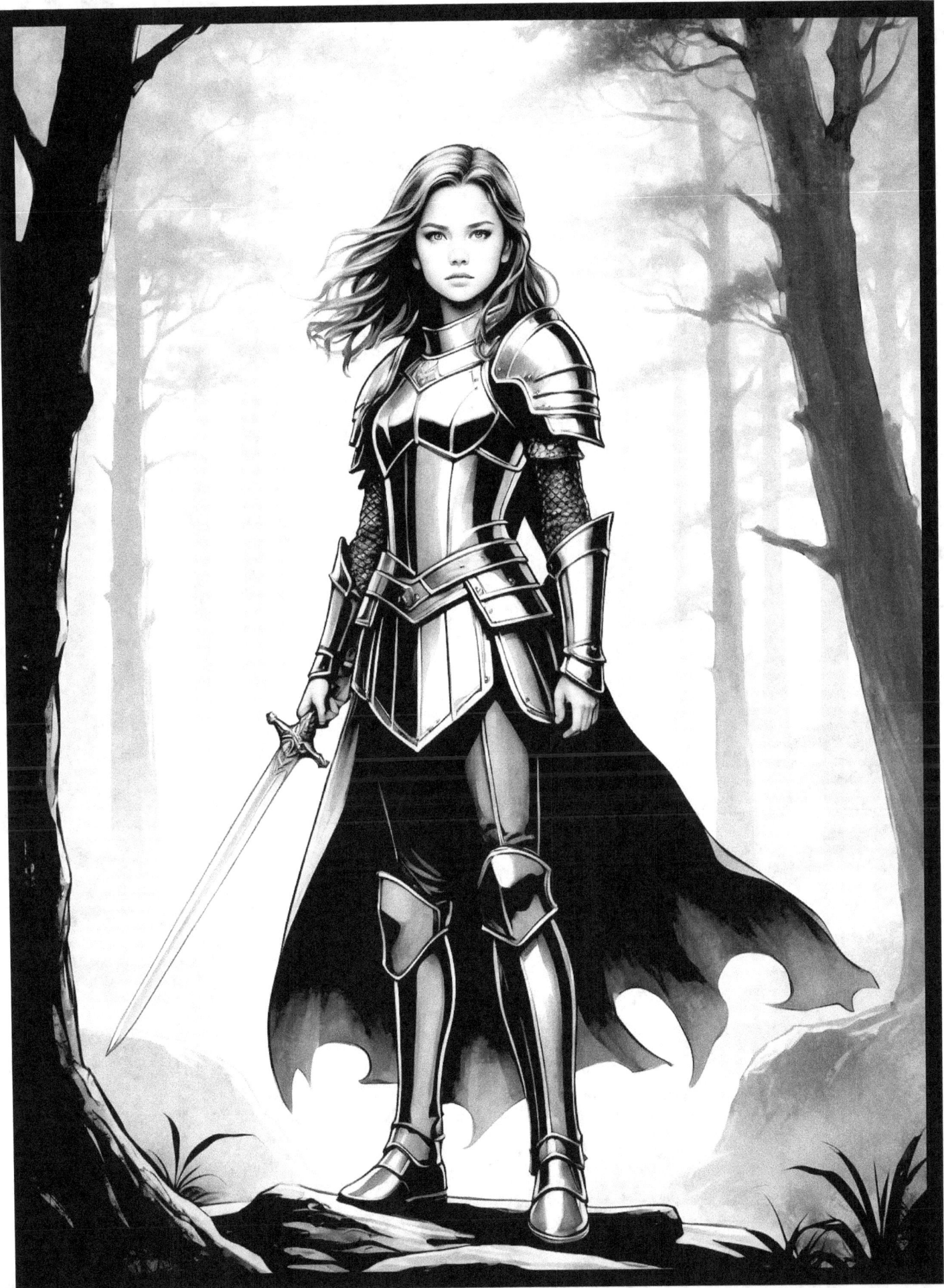

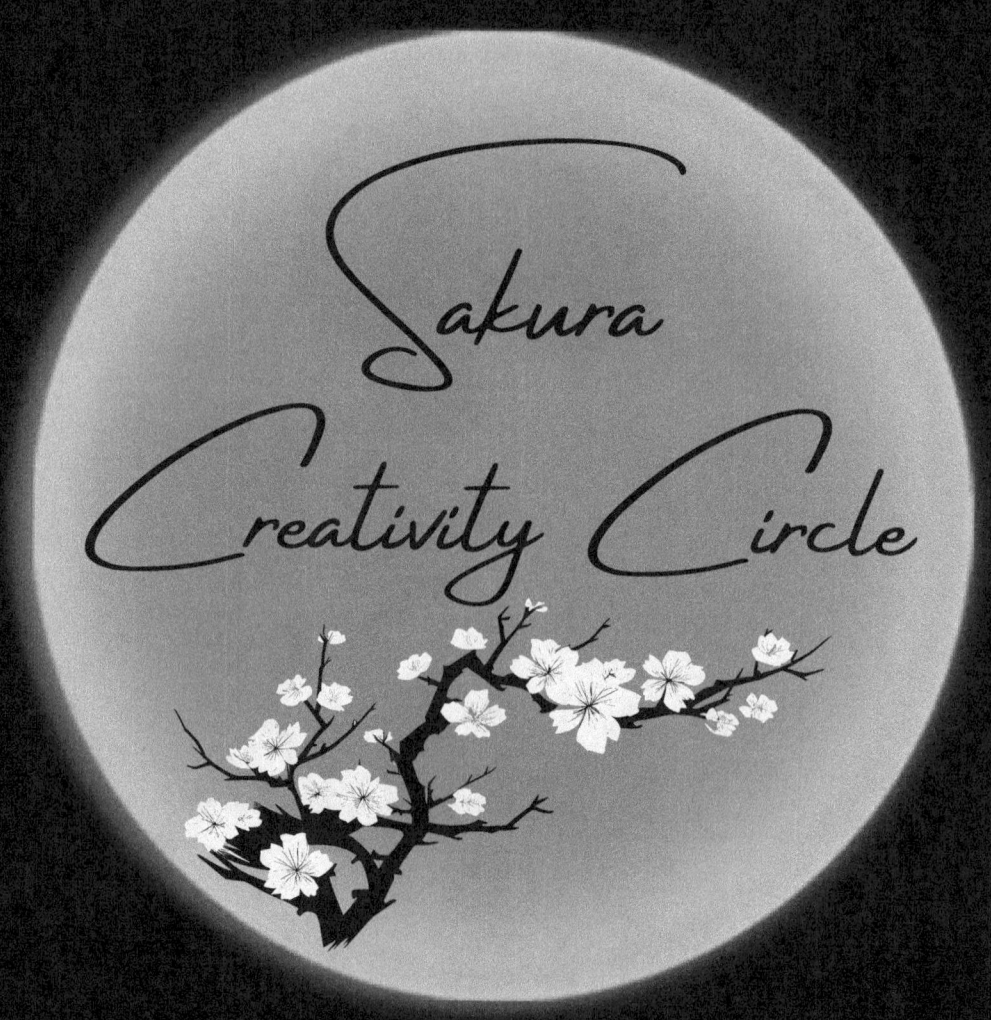

sakuracreativitycircle.com

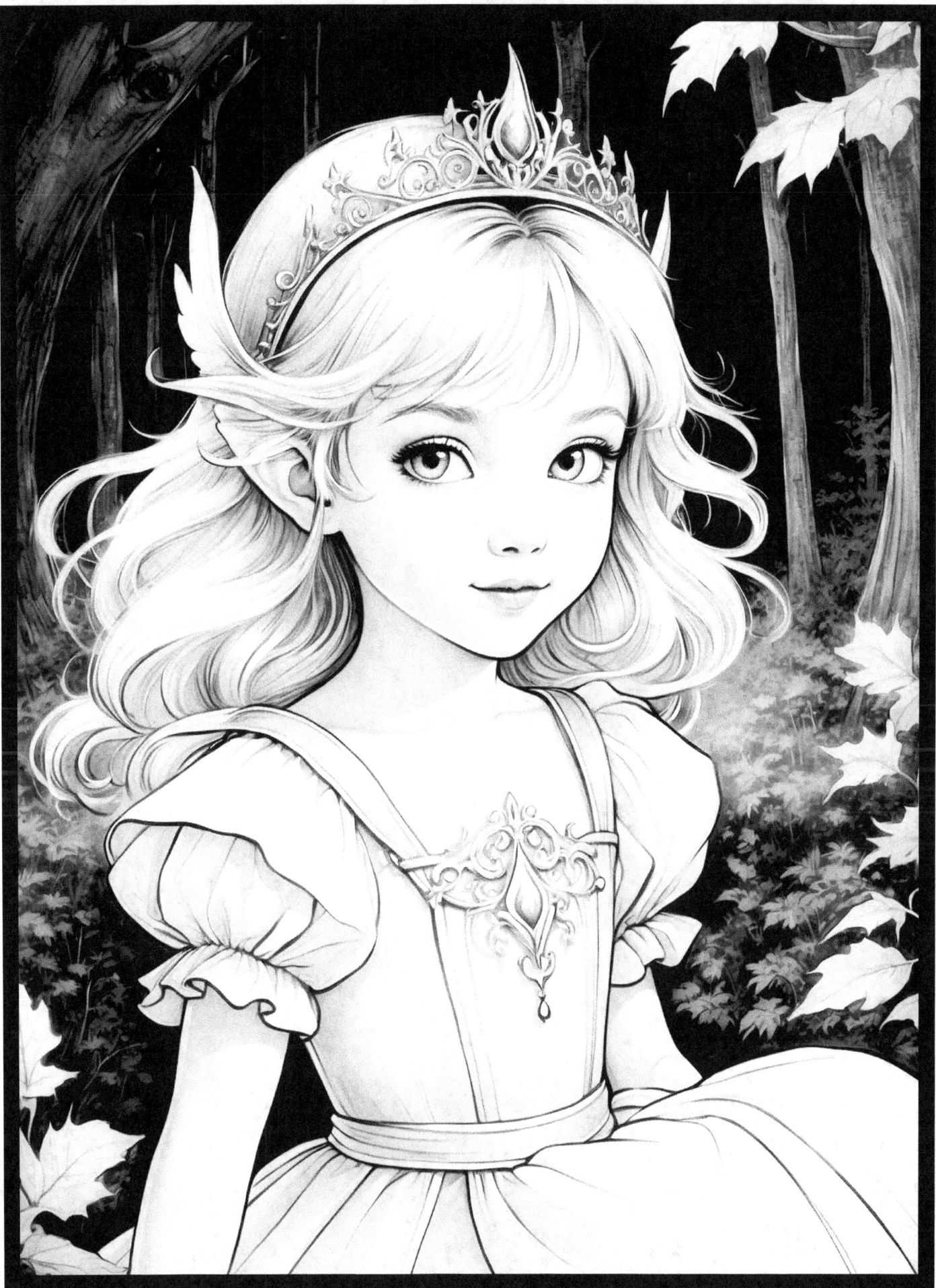

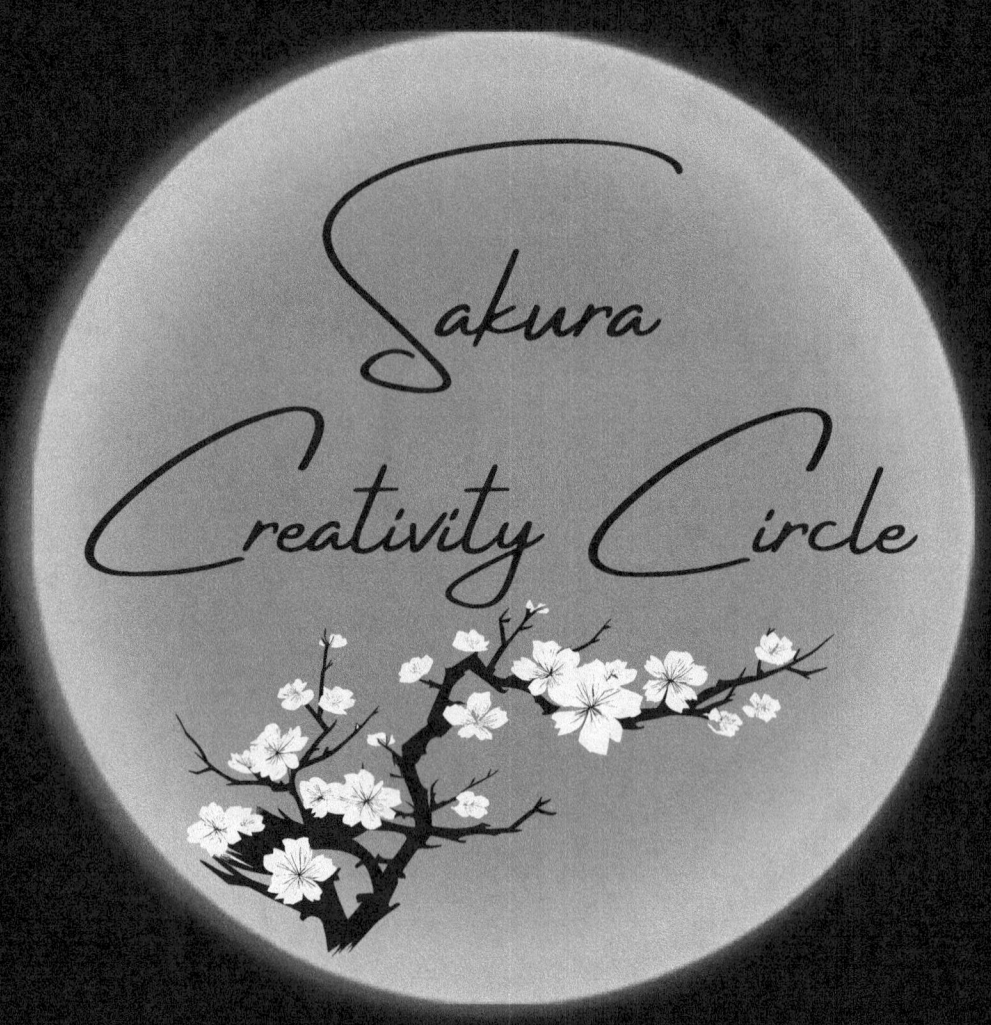

sakuracreativitycircle.com

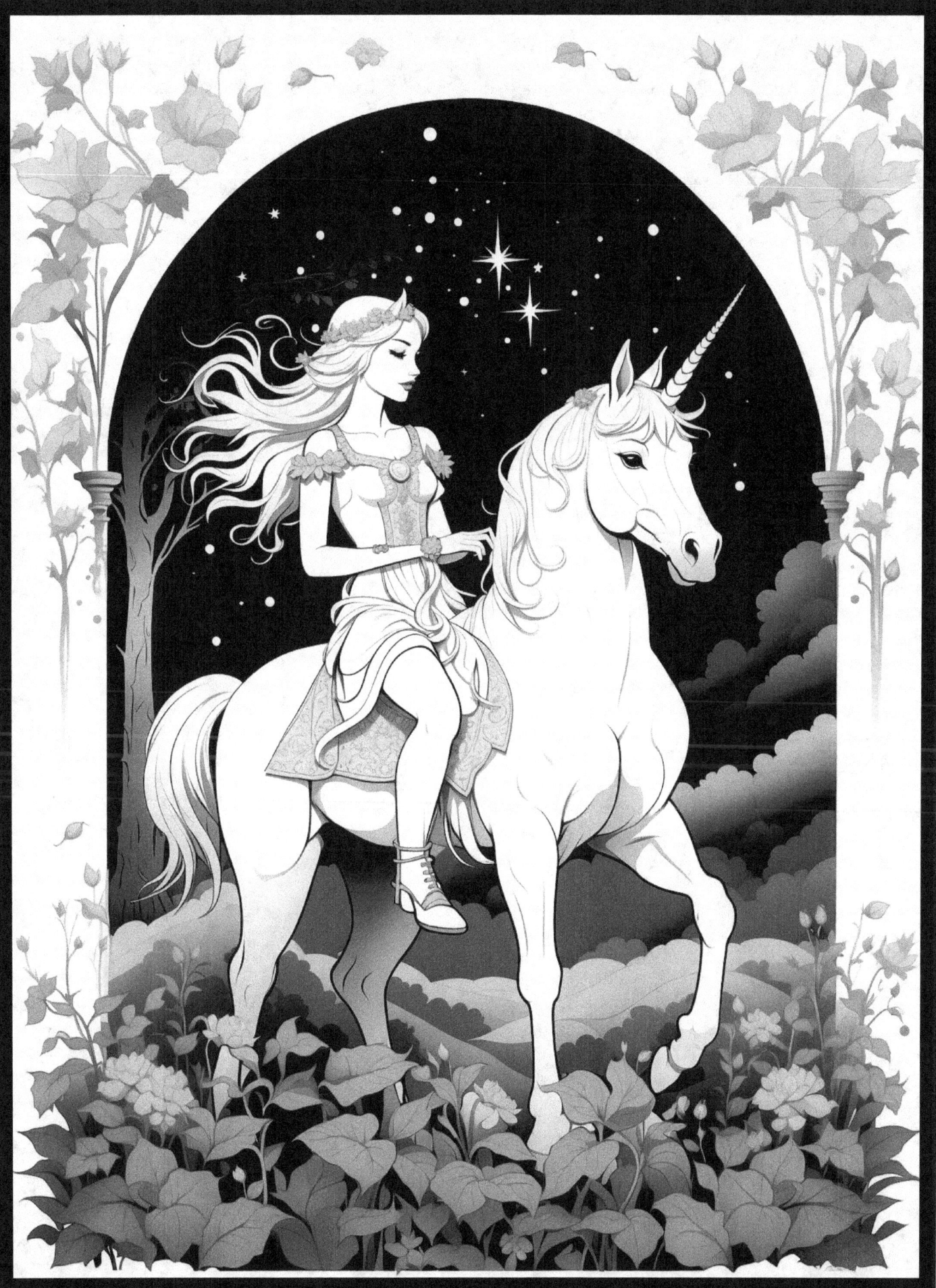

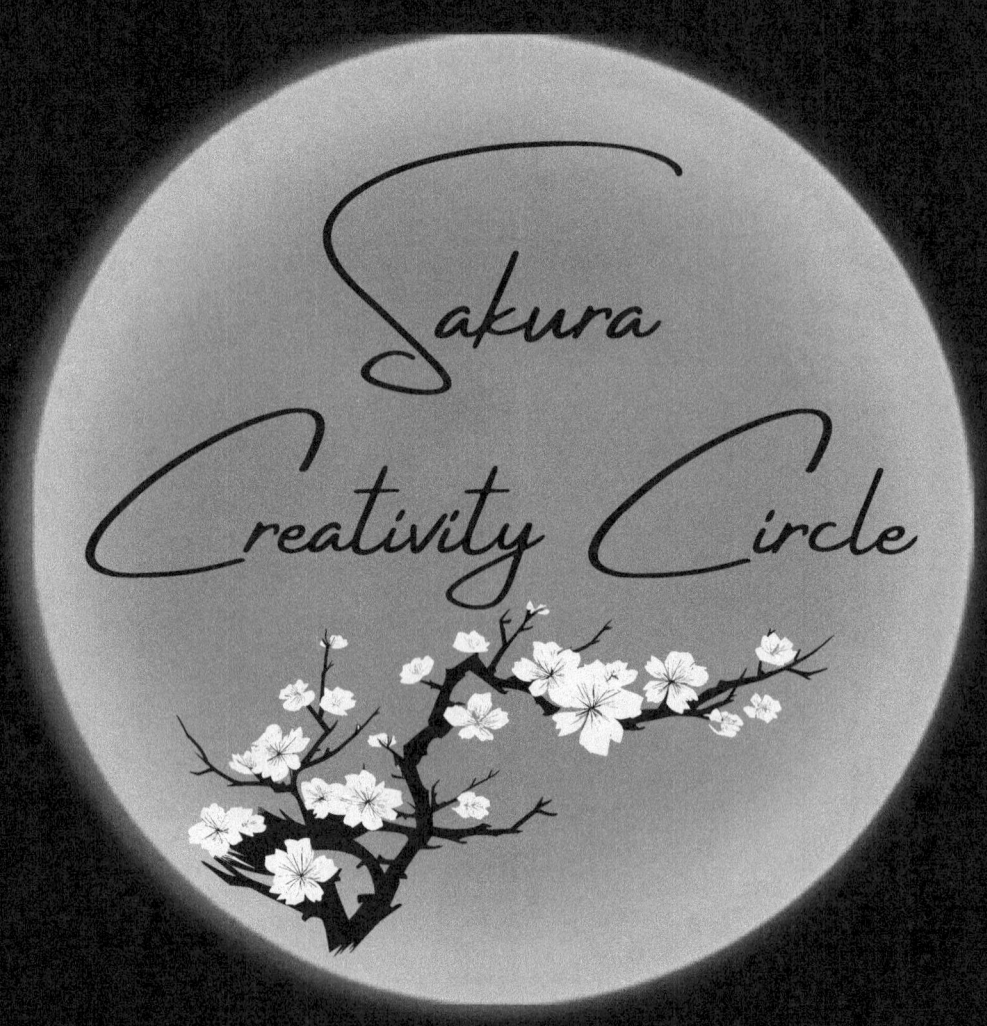

sakuracreativitycircle.com

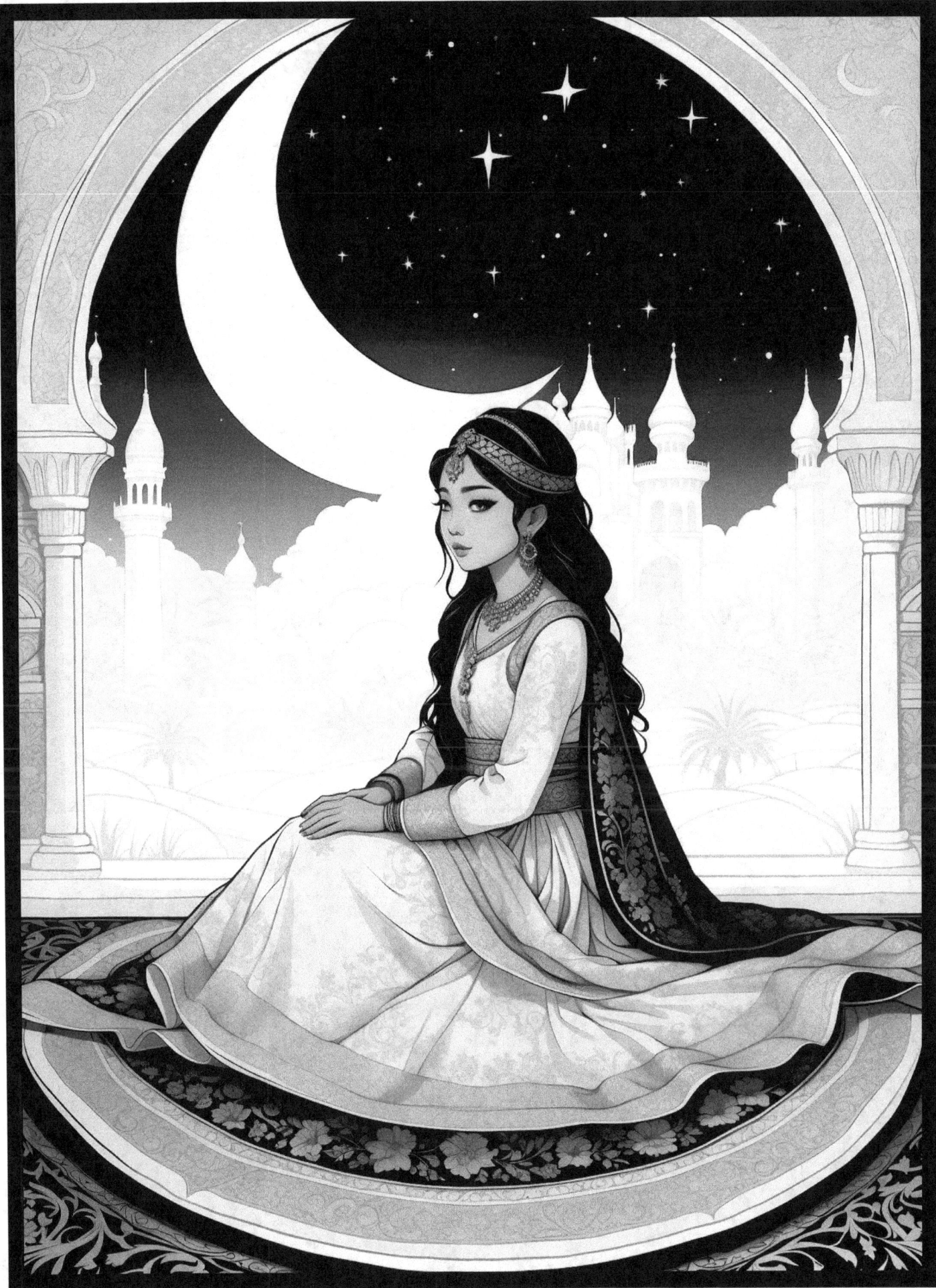

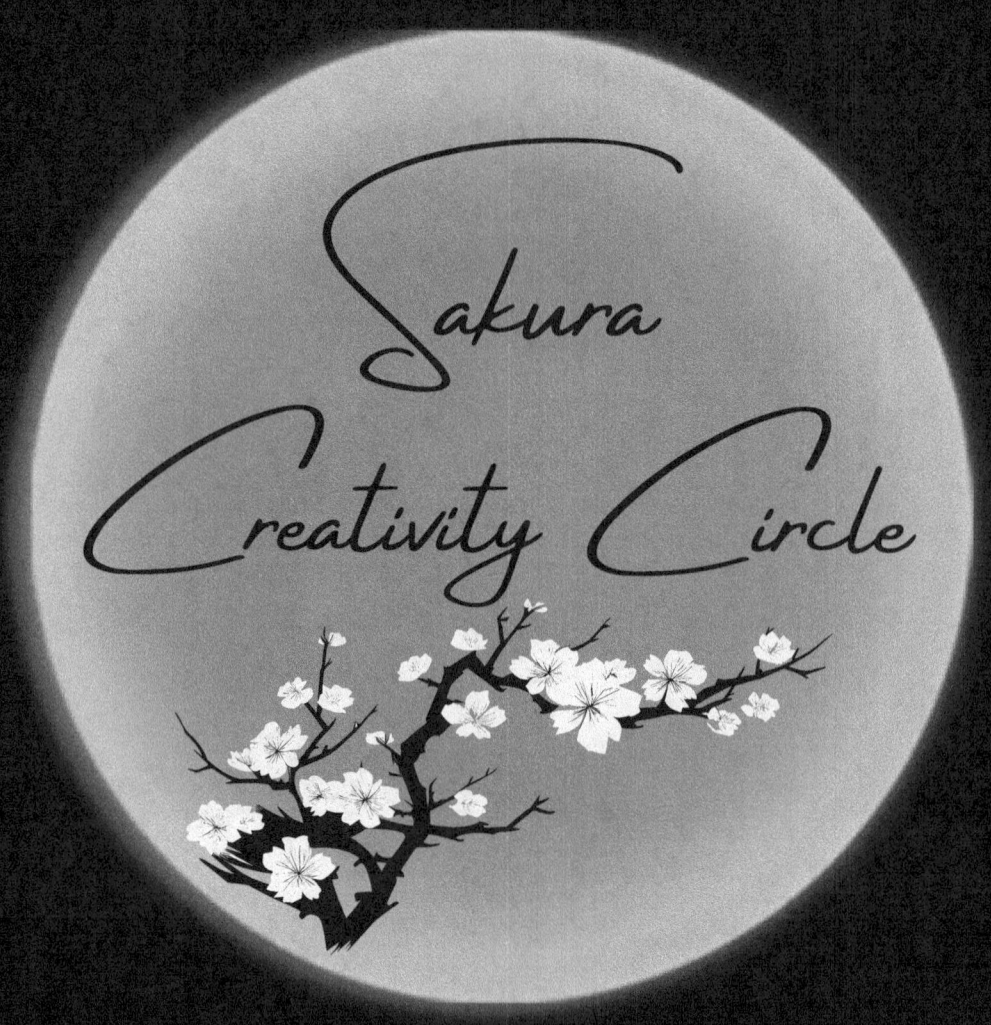

sakuracreativitycircle.com

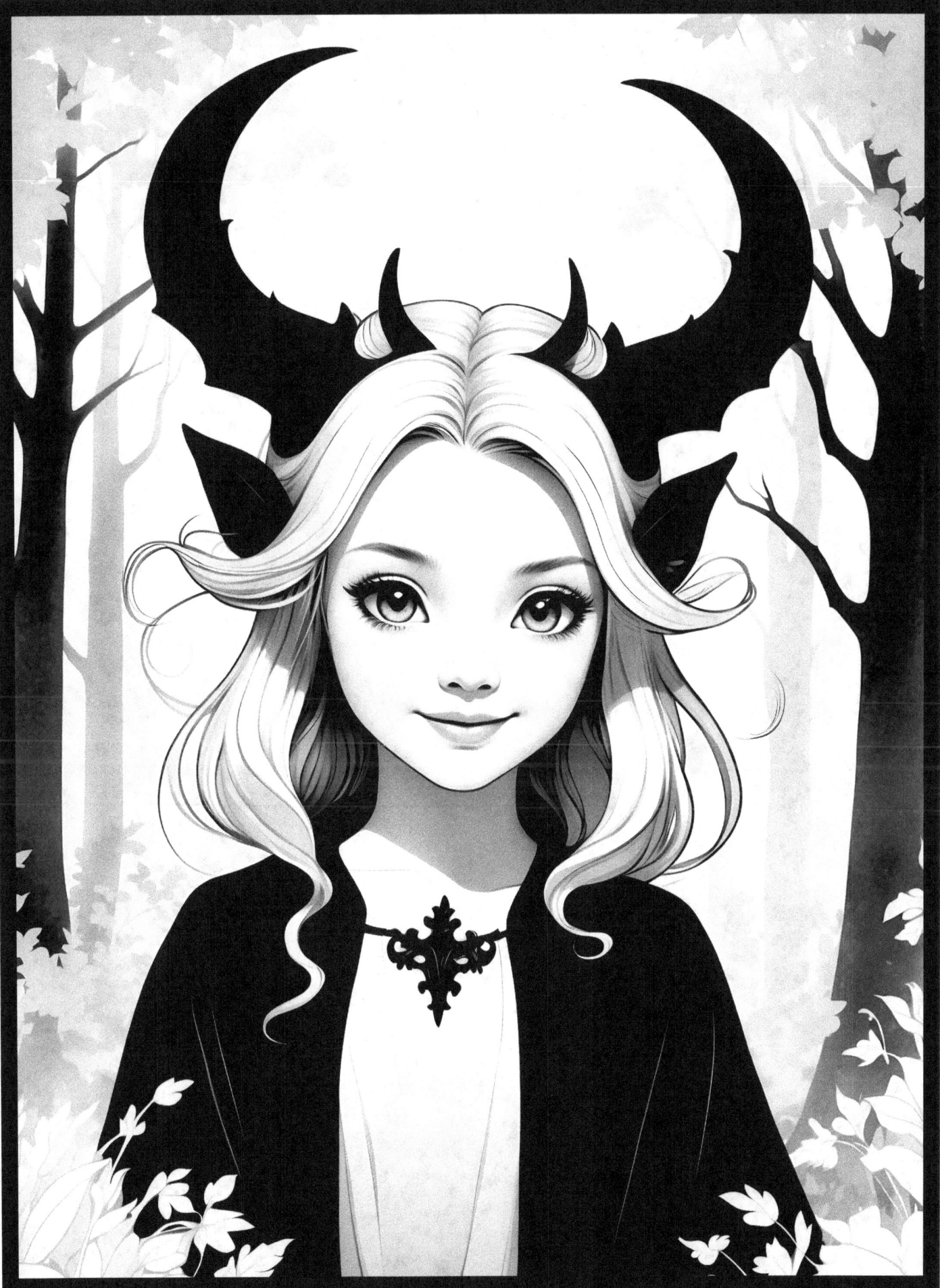

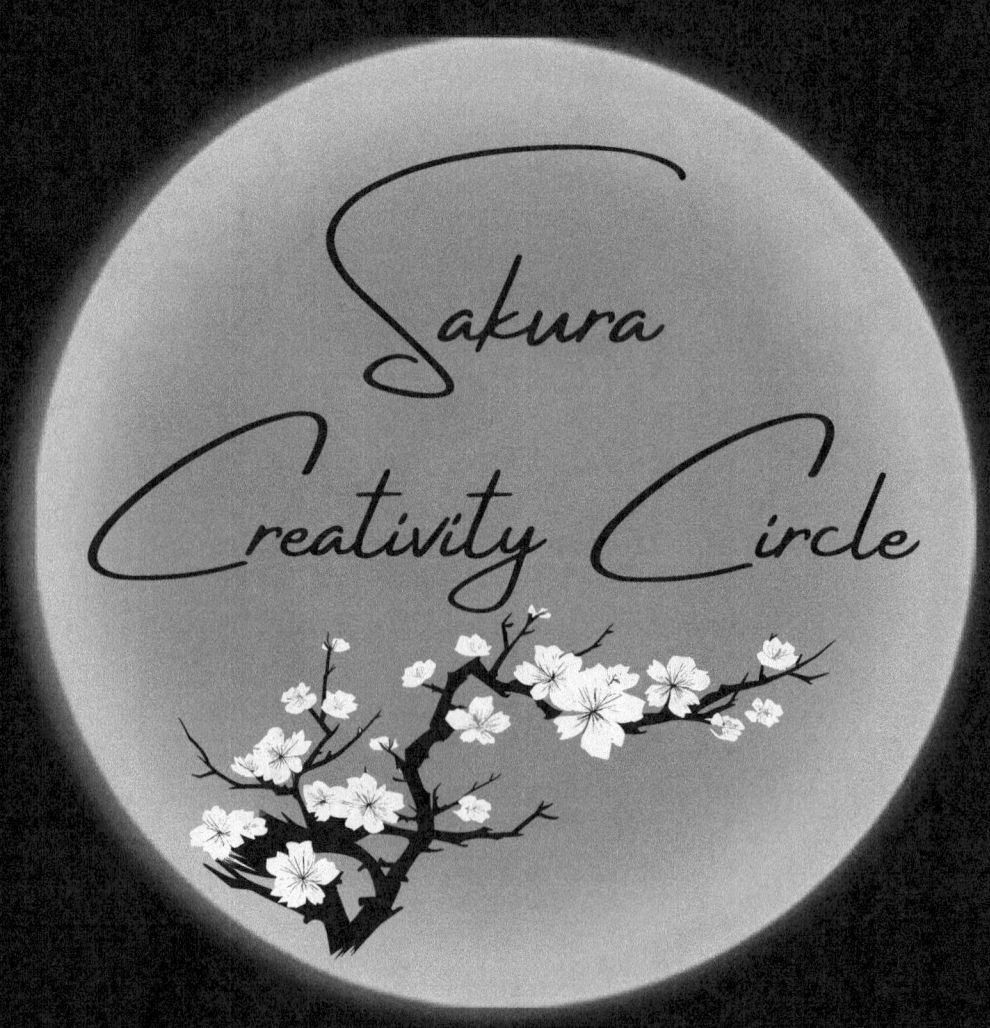

sakuracreativitycircle.com

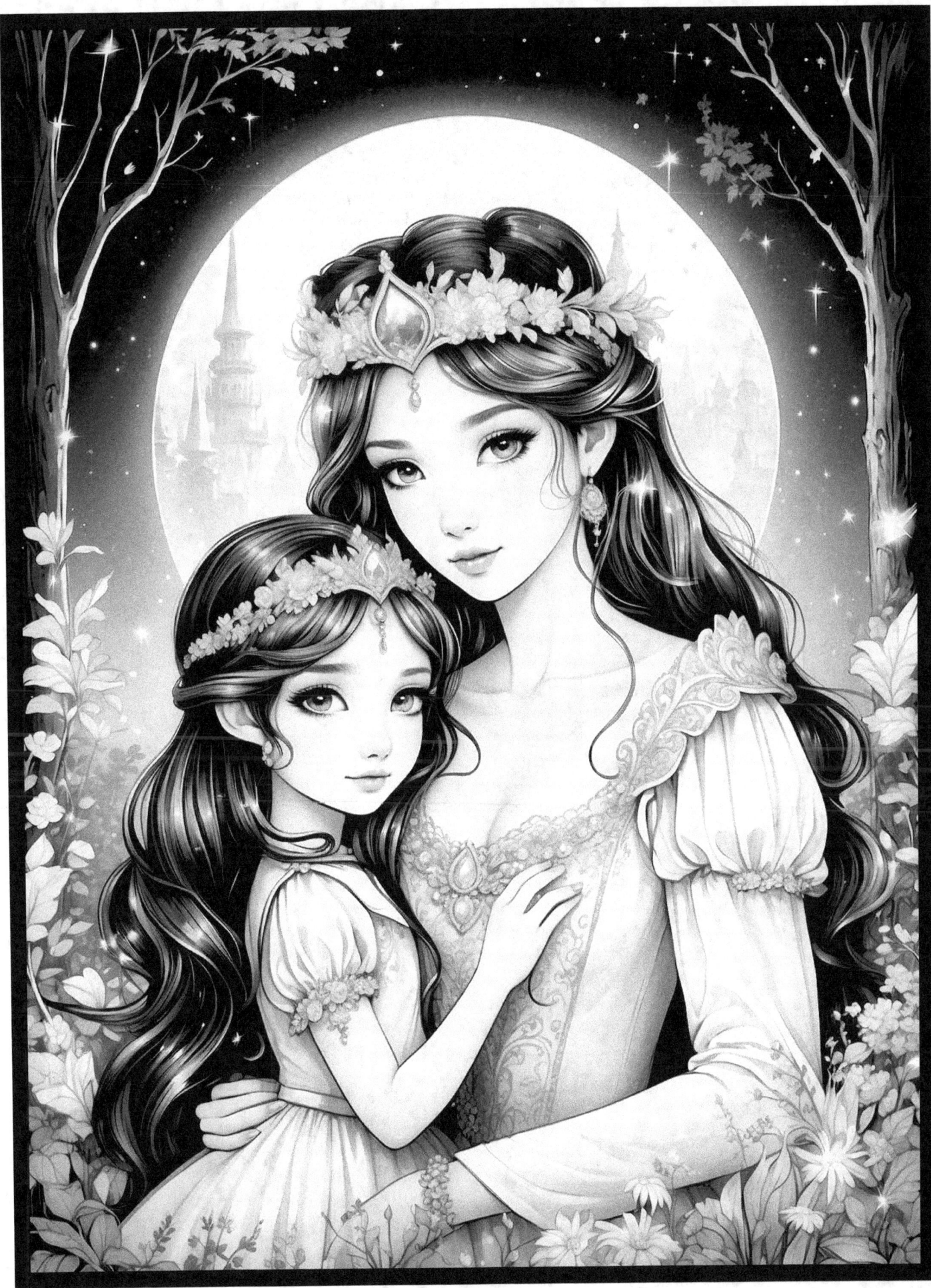

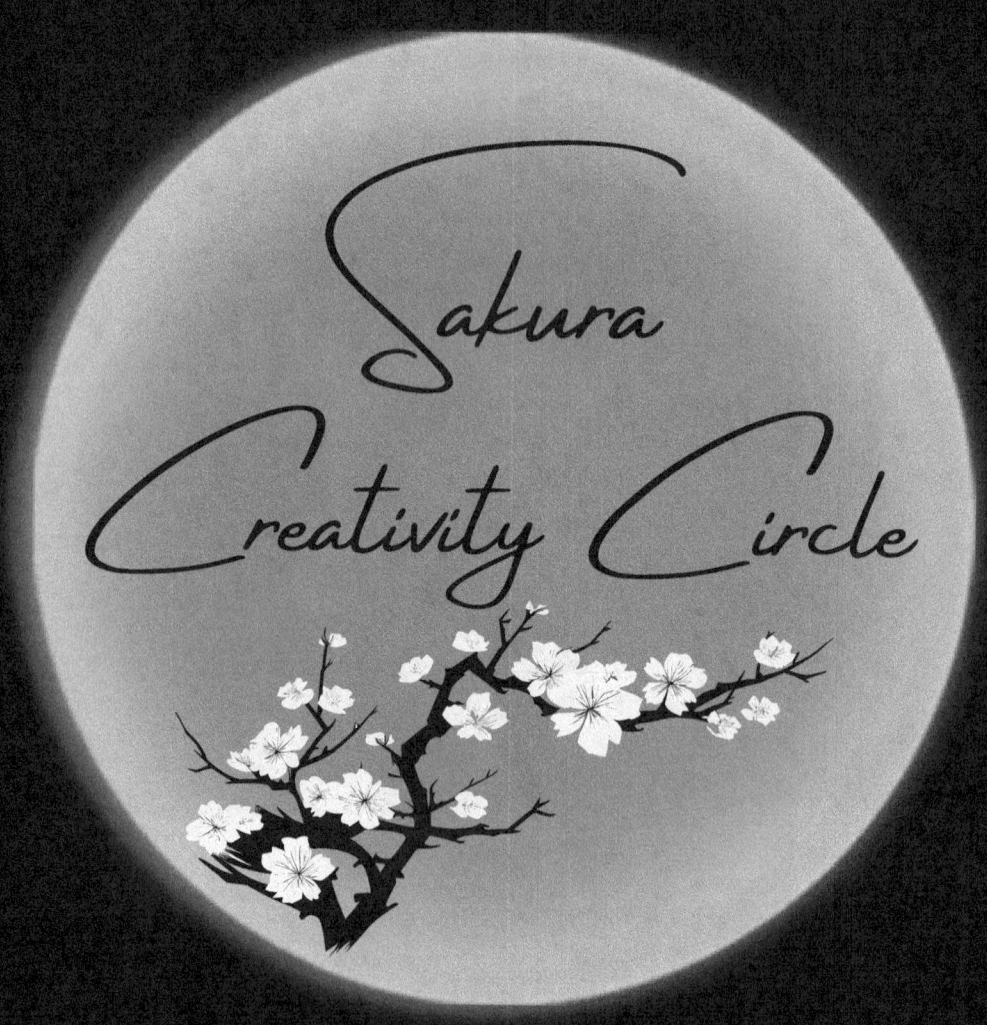

sakuracreativitycircle.com

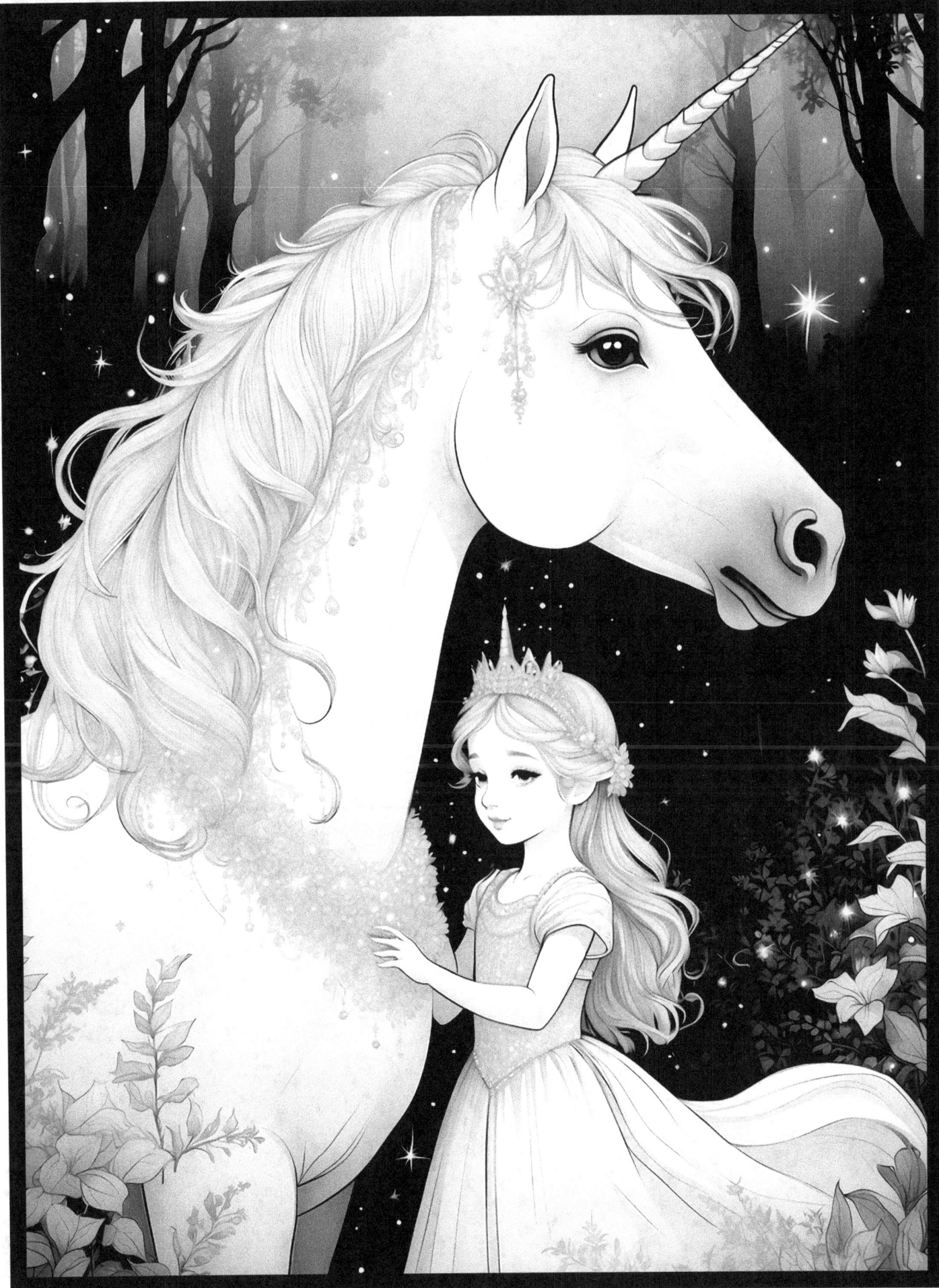

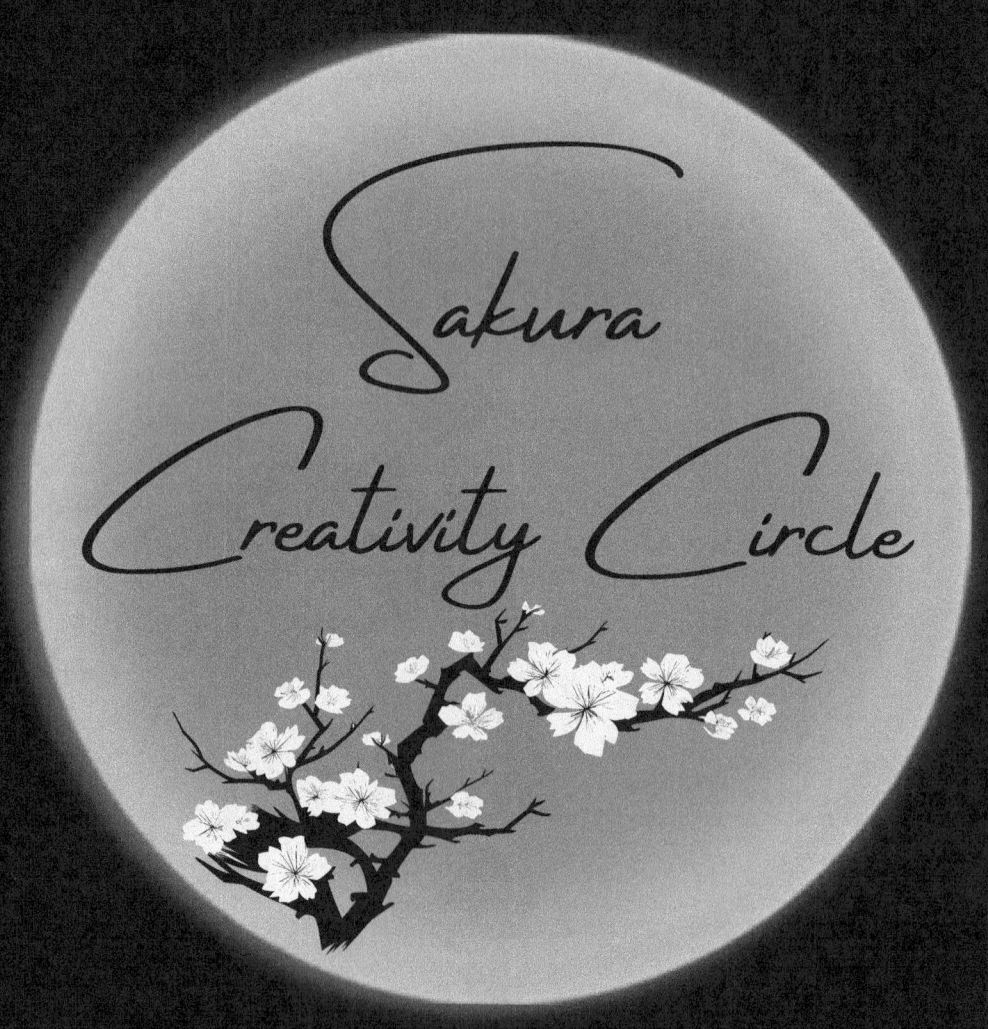

sakuracreativitycircle.com

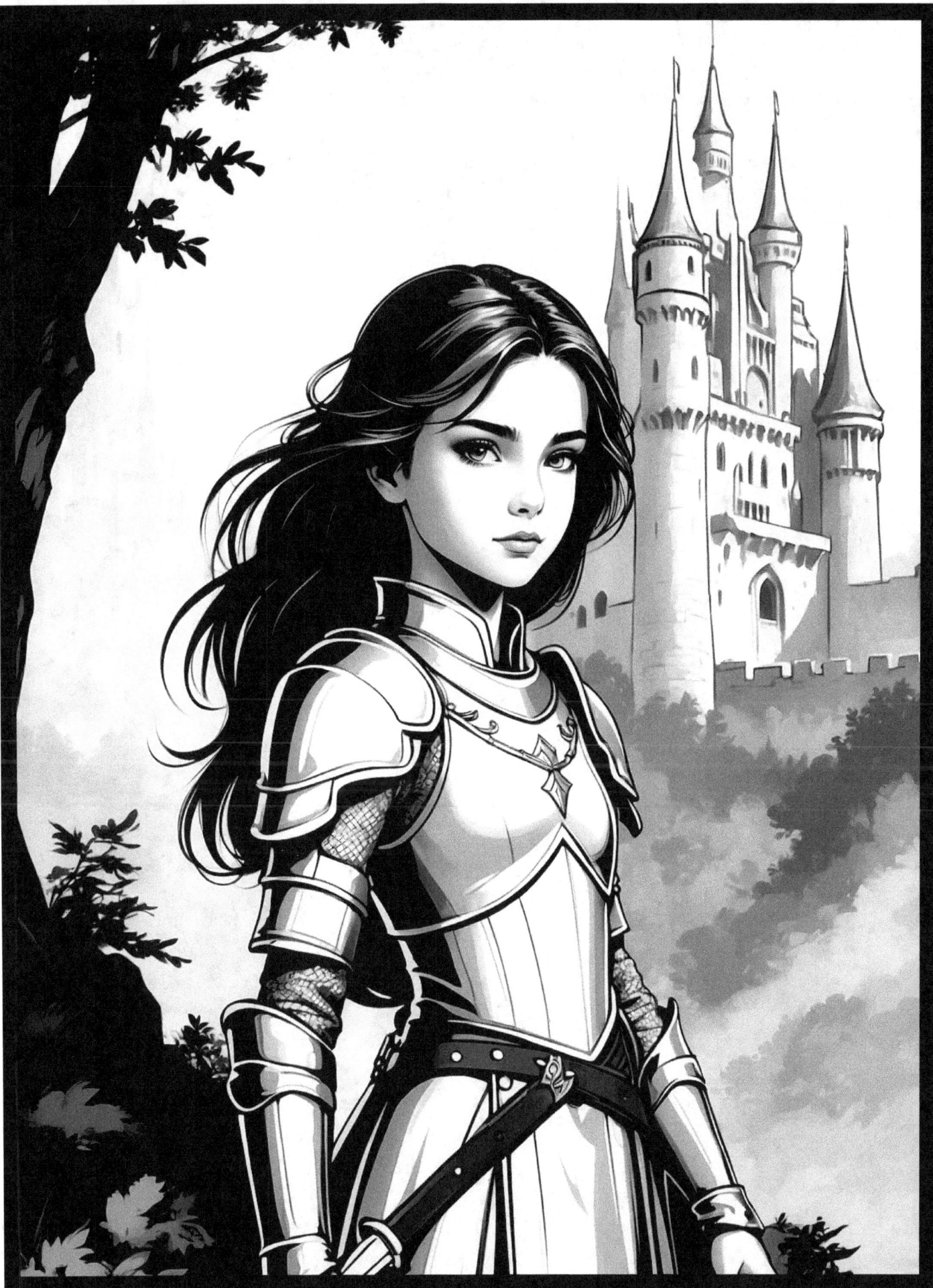

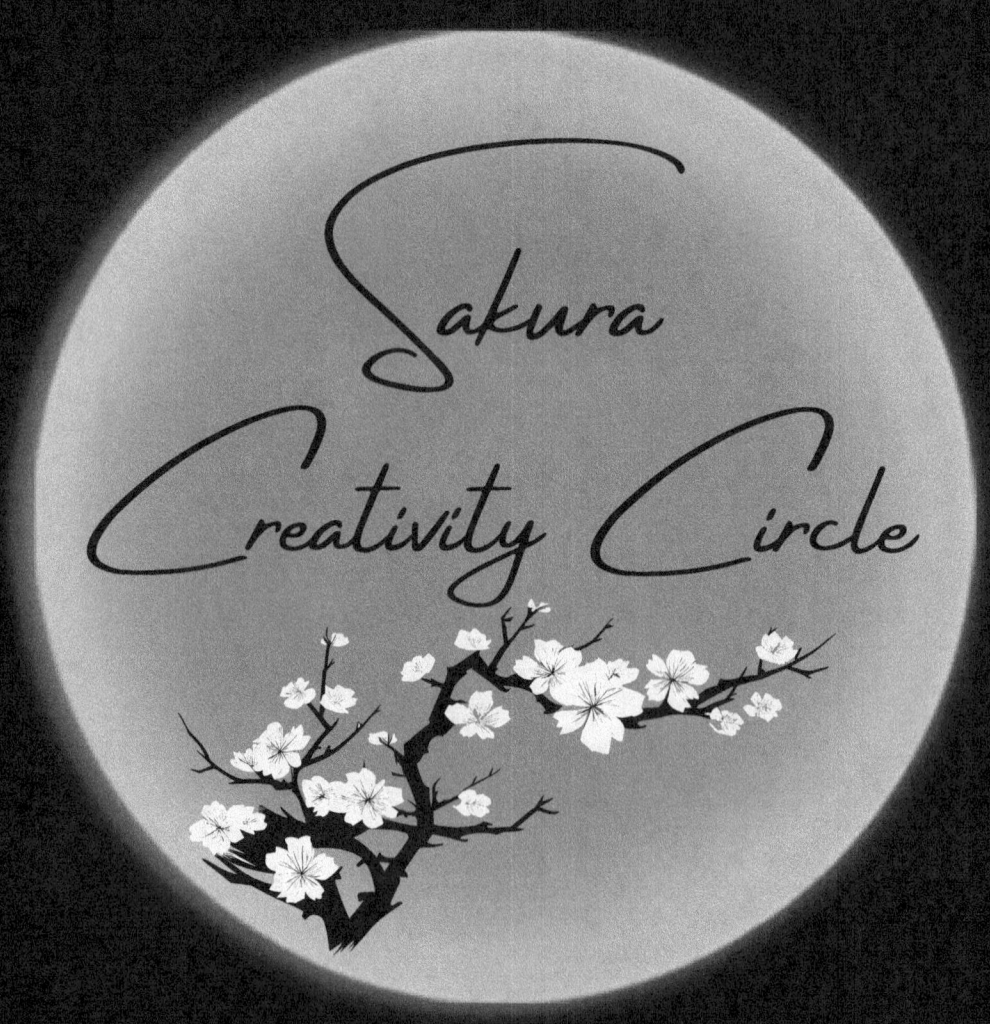

sakuracreativitycircle.com

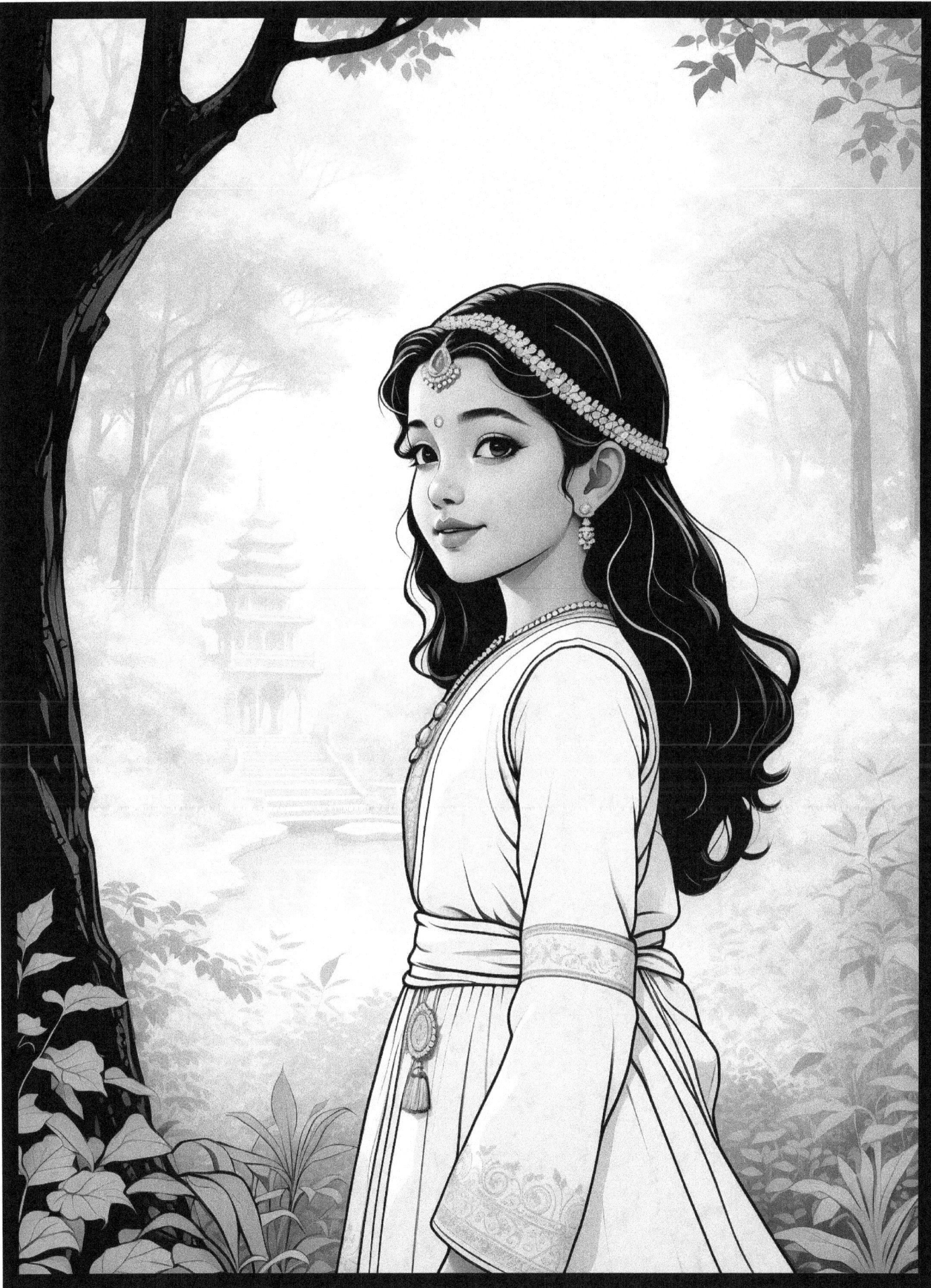

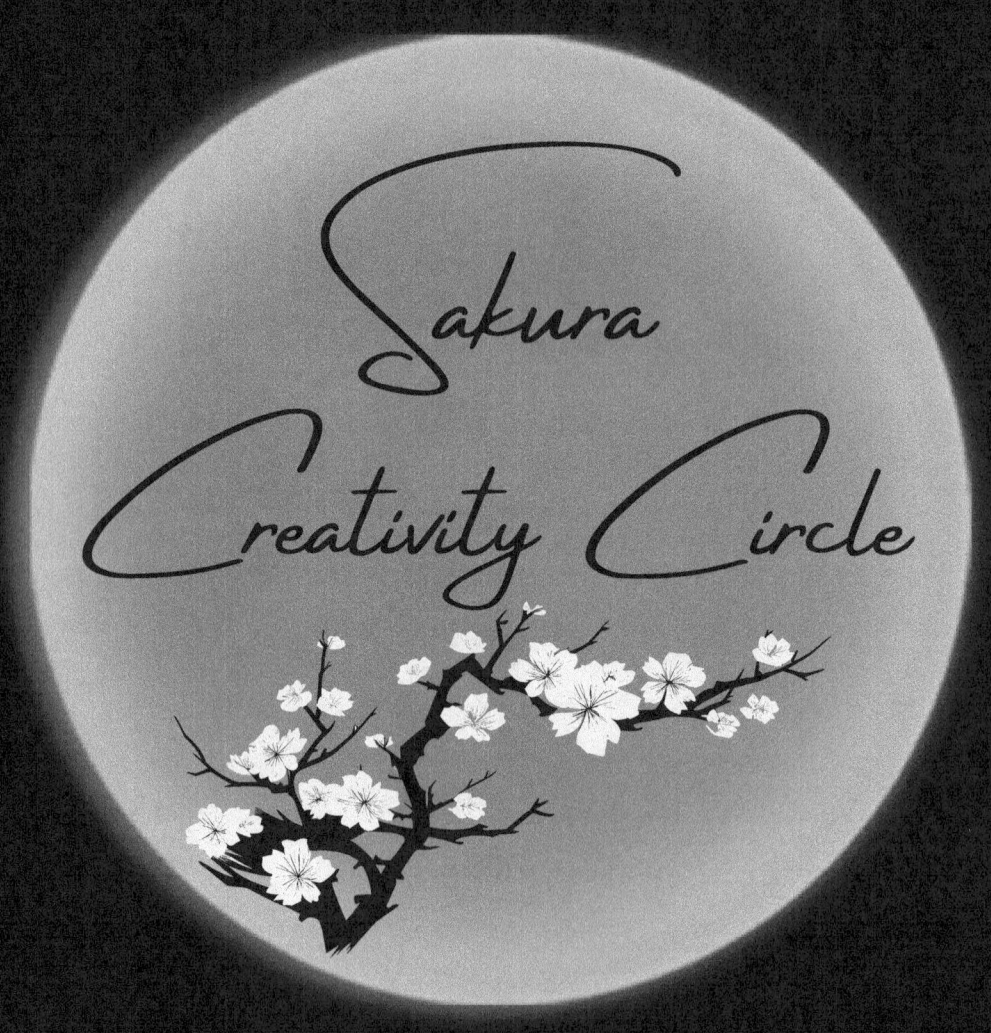

sakuracreativitycircle.com

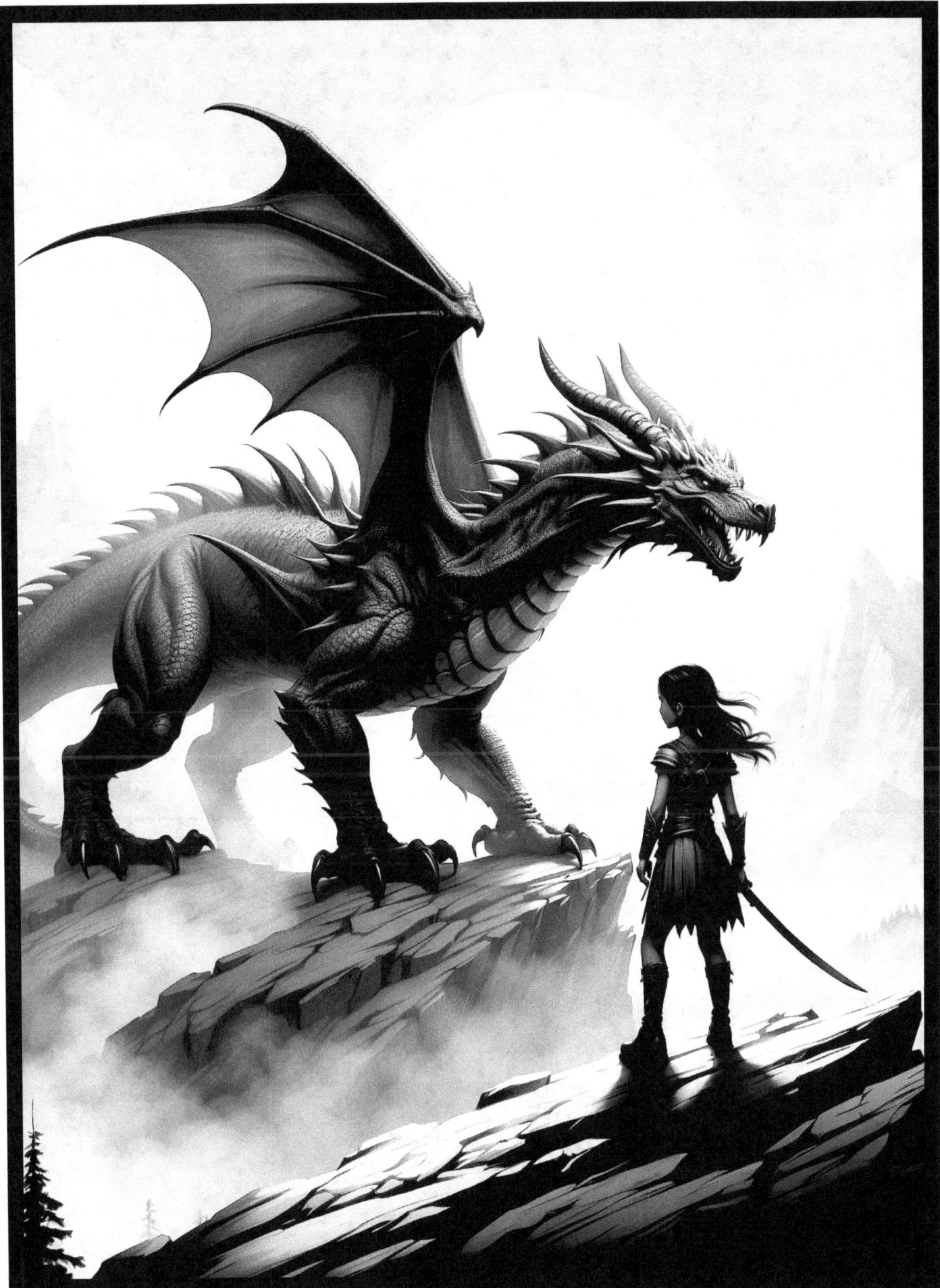

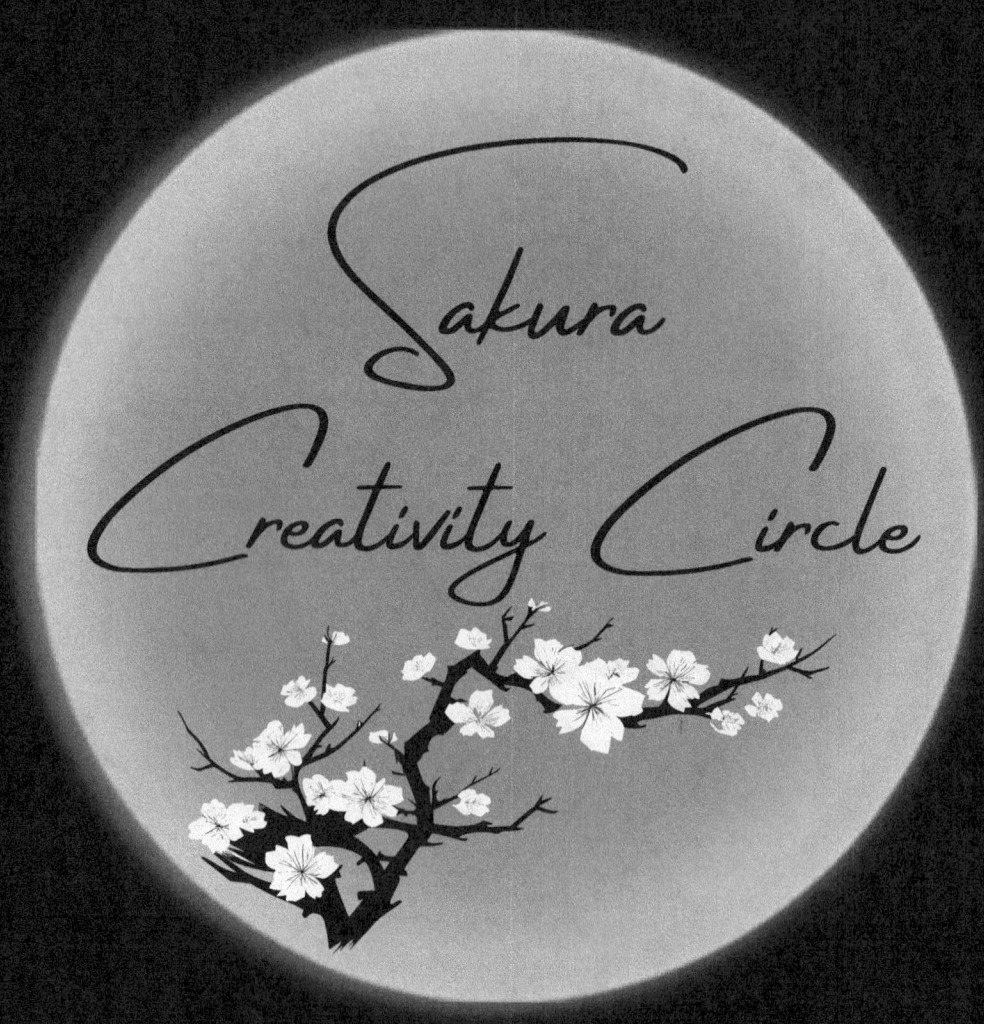

sakuracreativitycircle.com

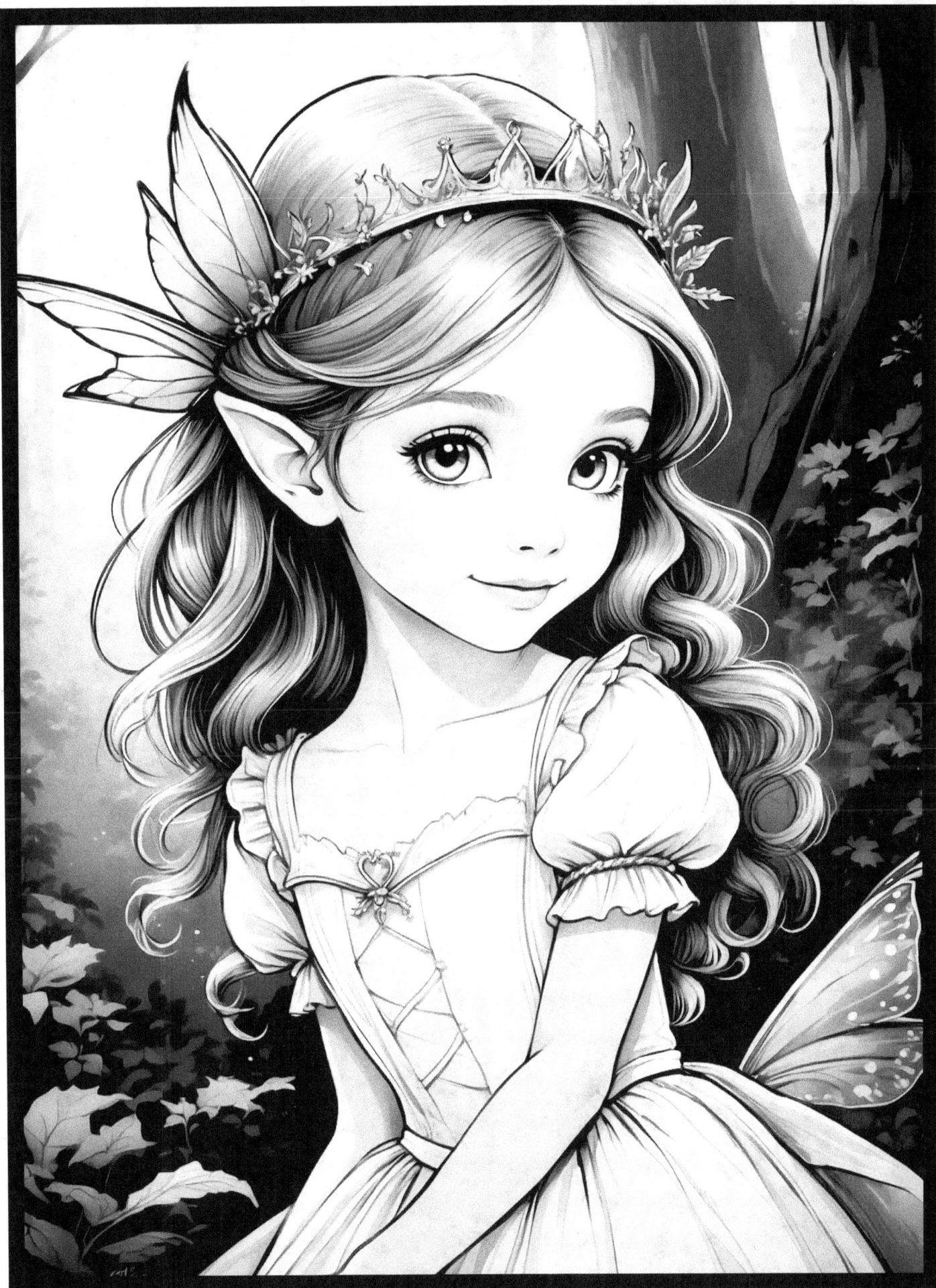

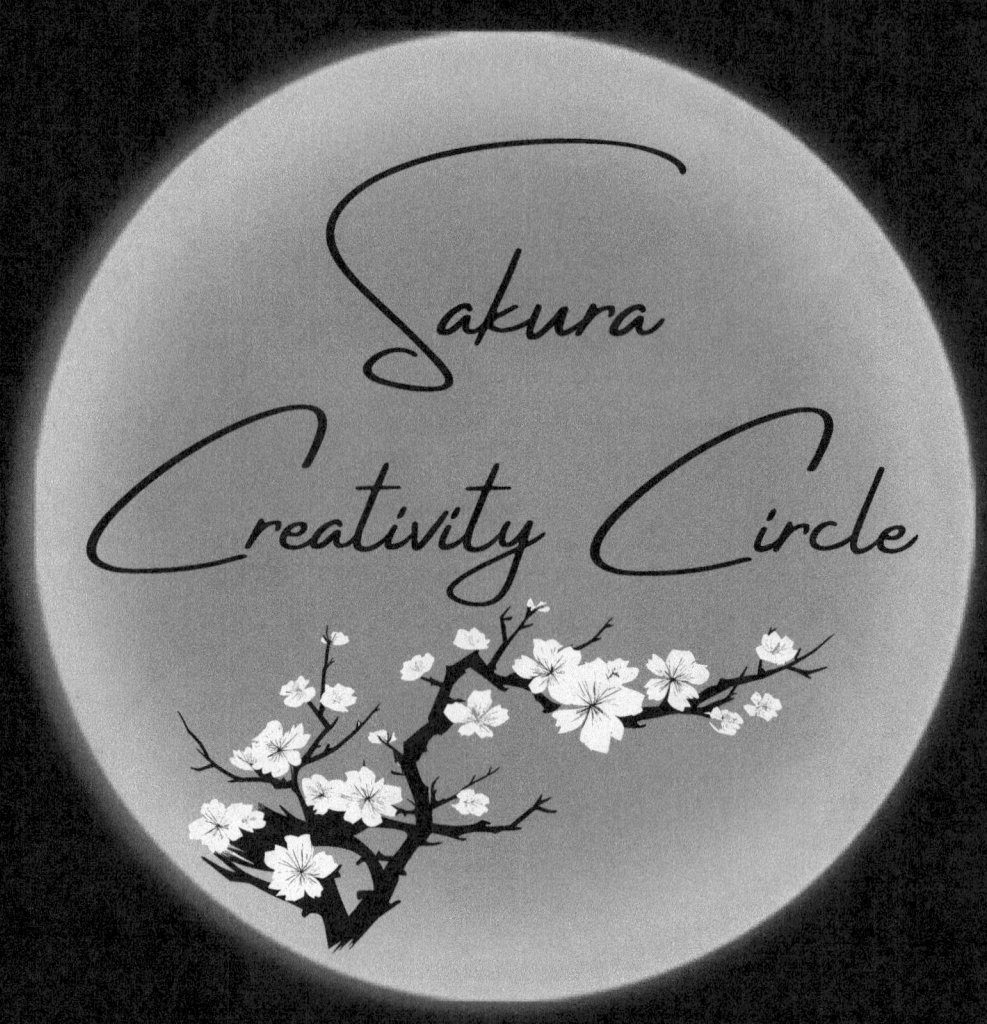

sakuracreativitycircle.com

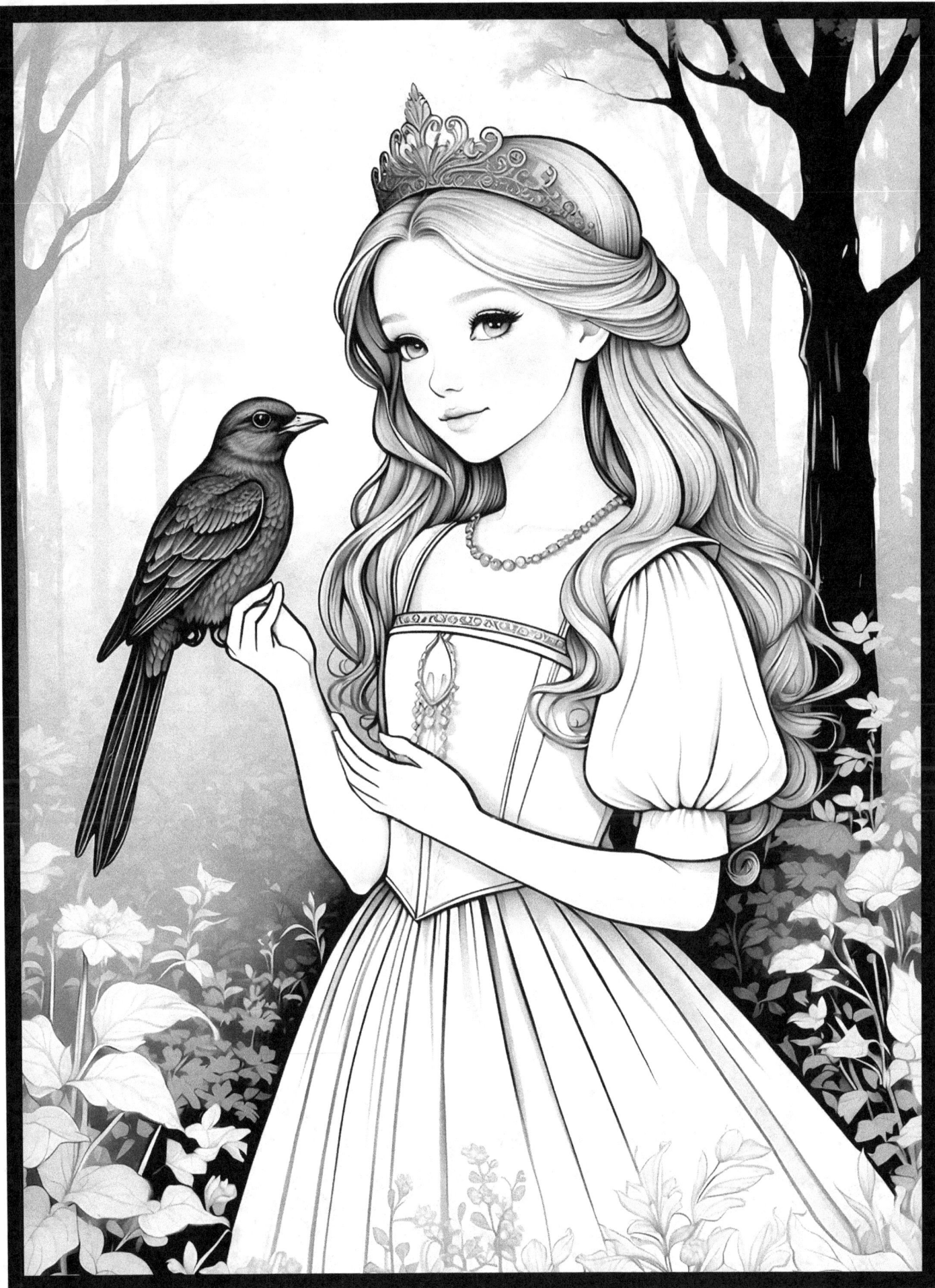

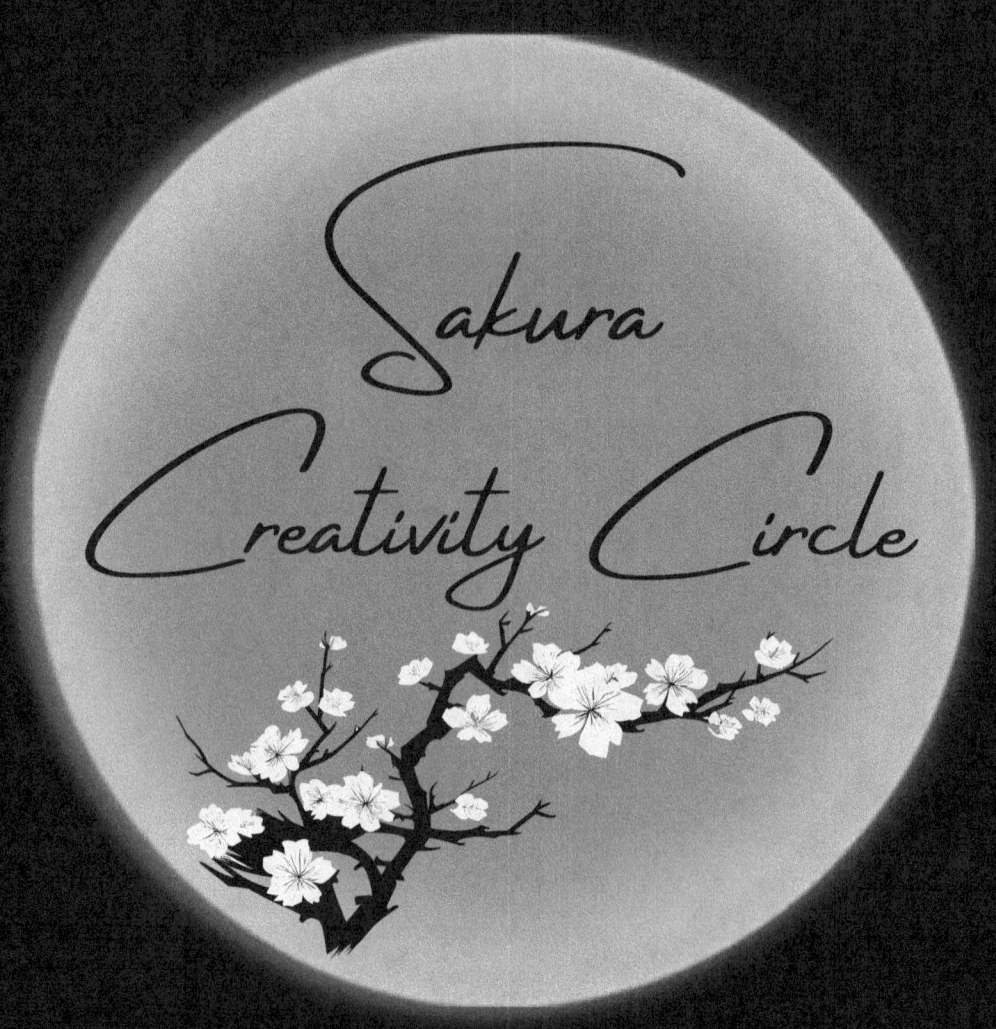

sakuracreativitycircle.com

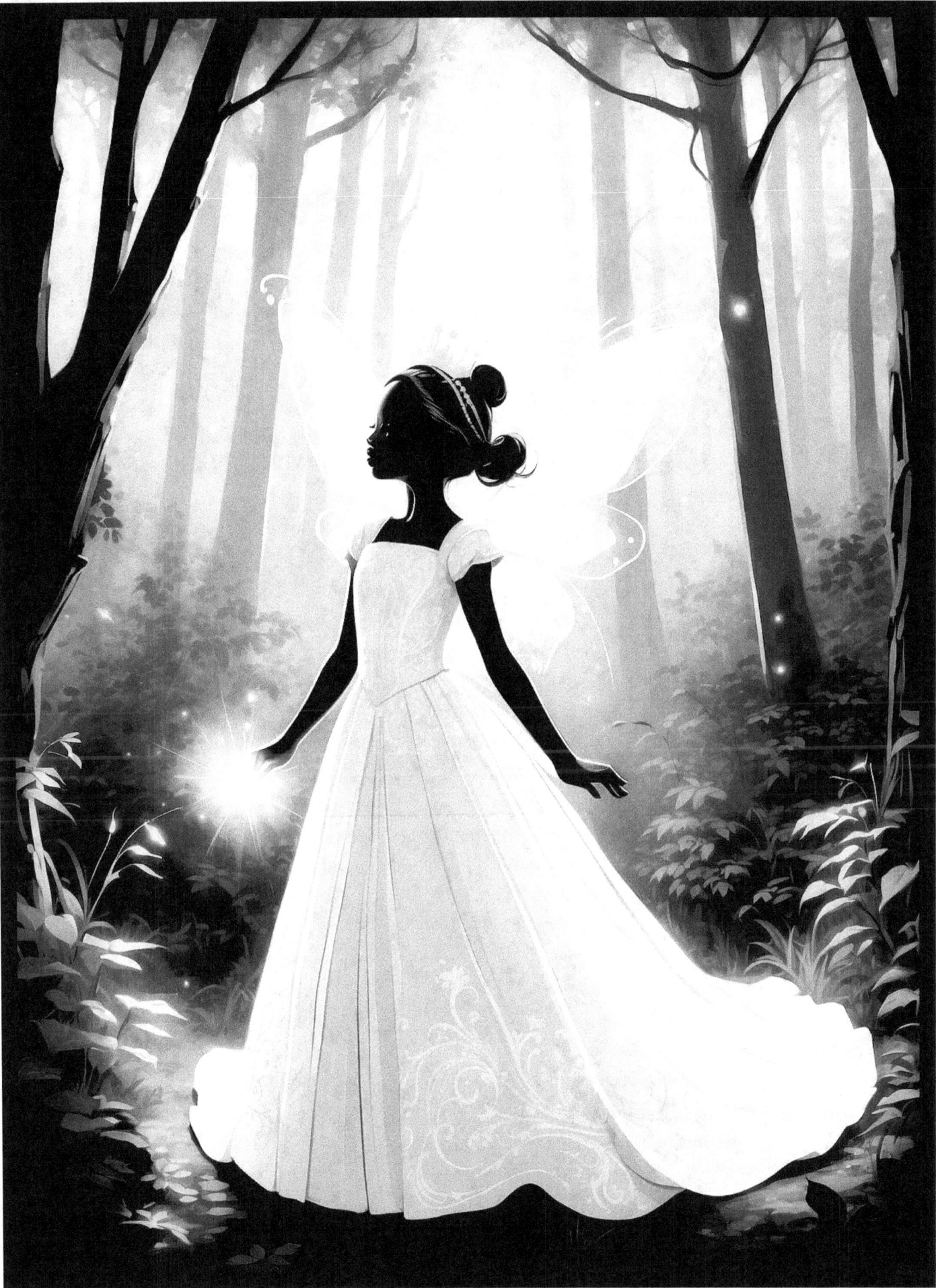

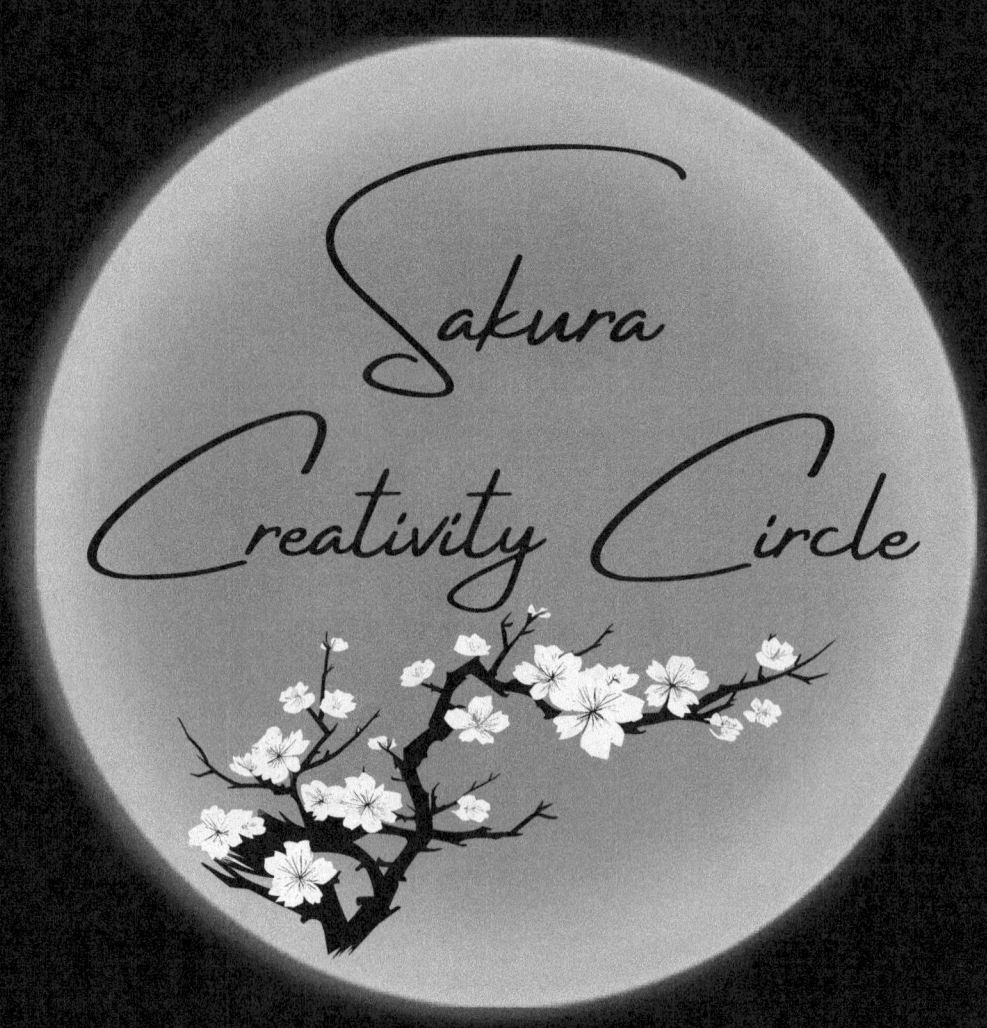

sakuracreativitycircle.com

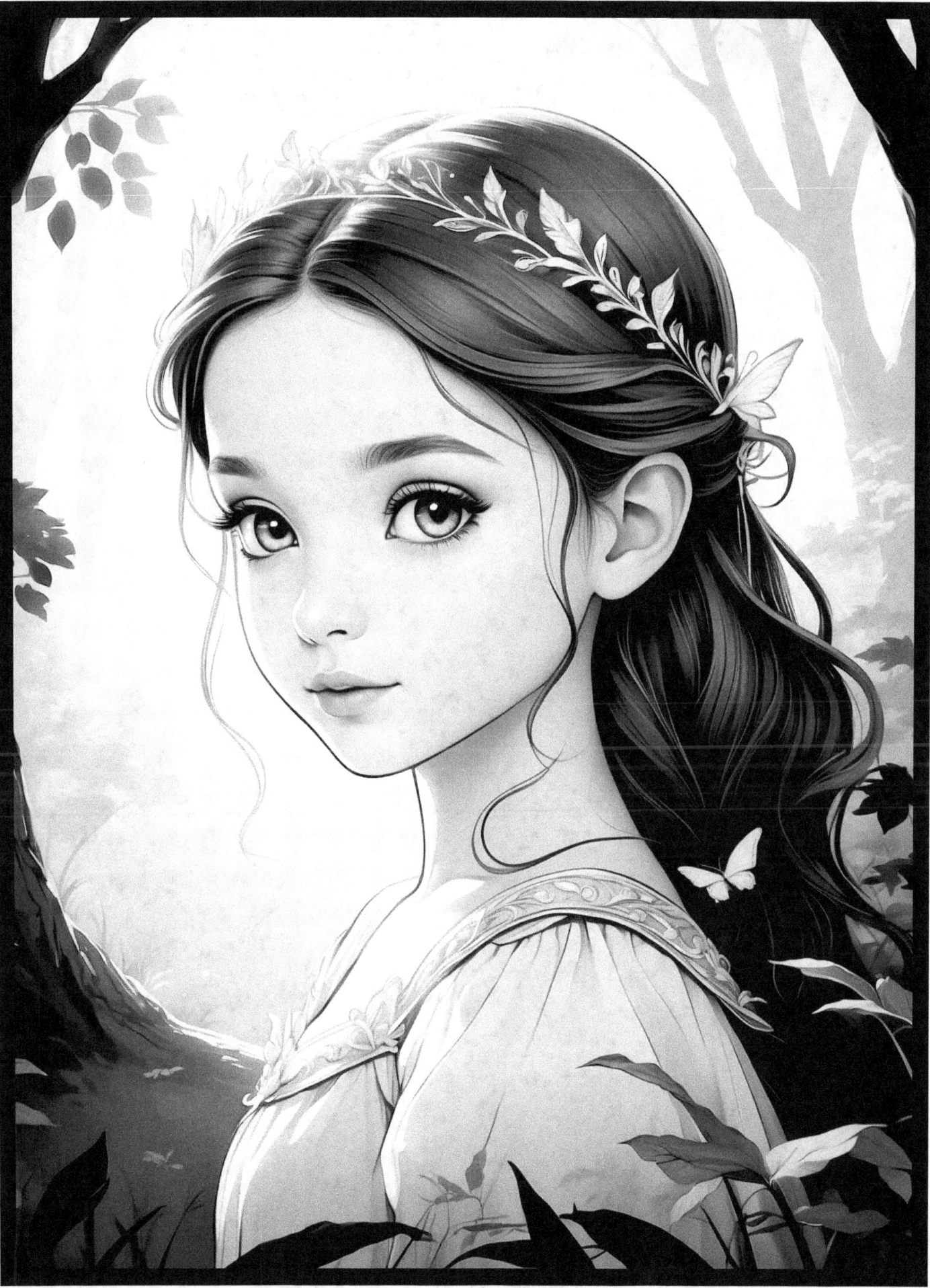

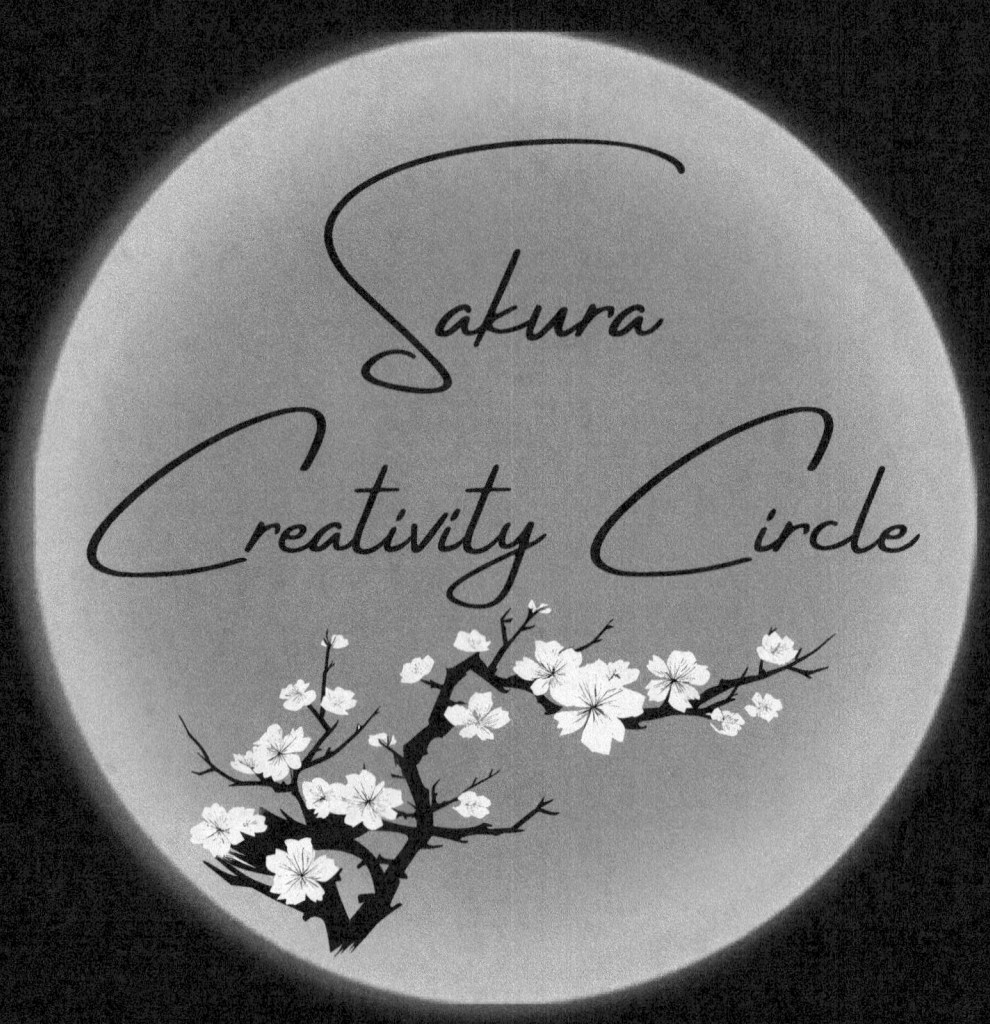

sakuracreativitycircle.com

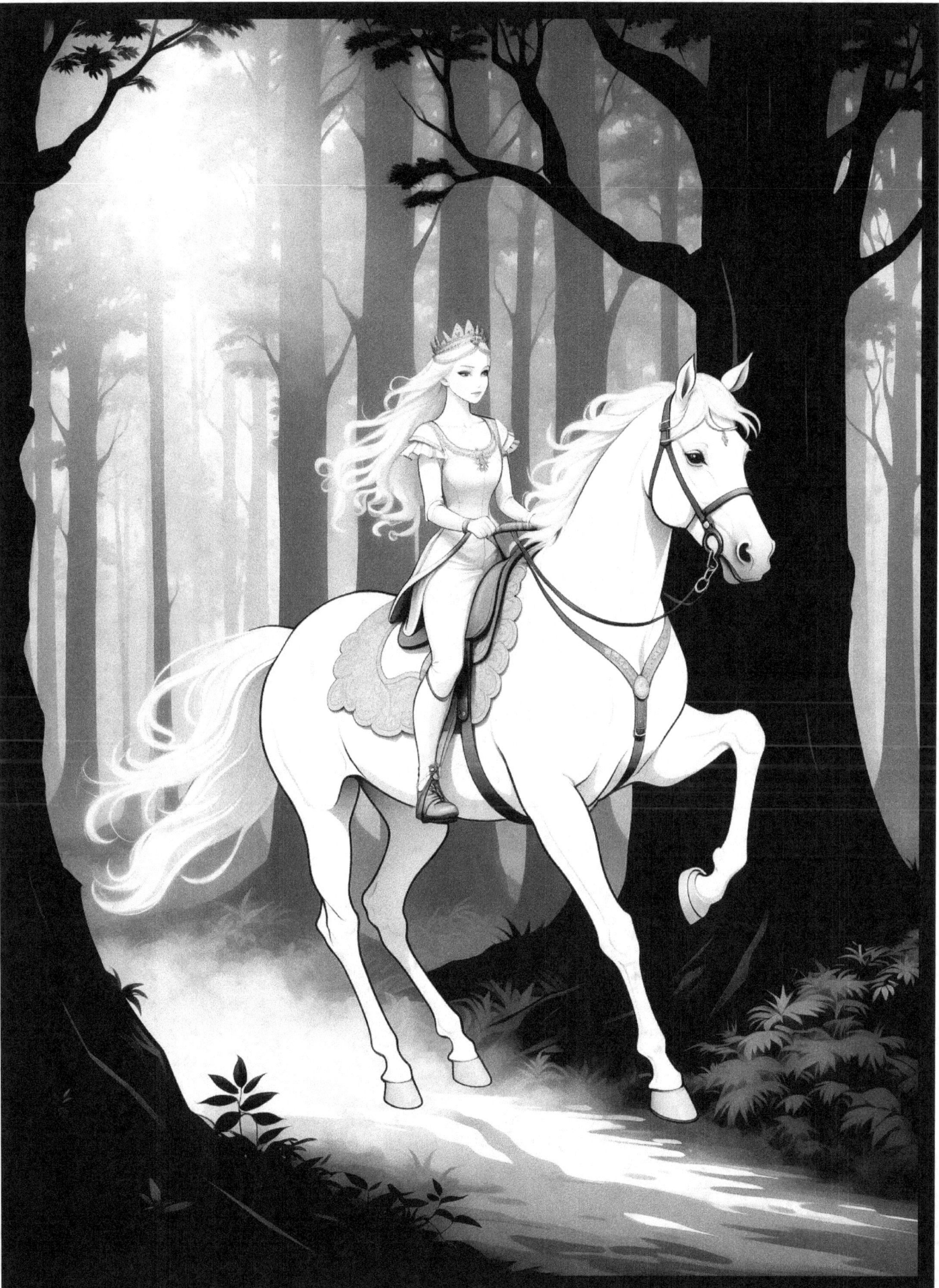

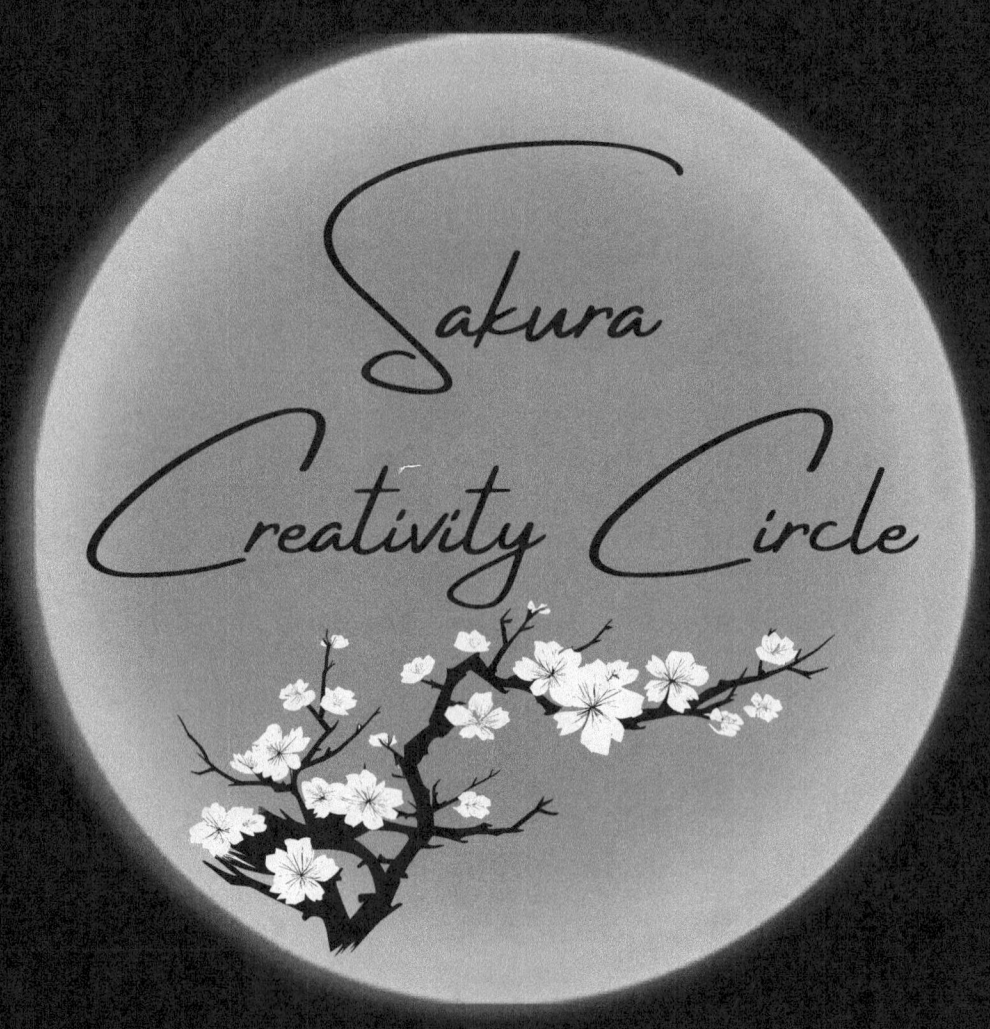

sakuracreativitycircle.com

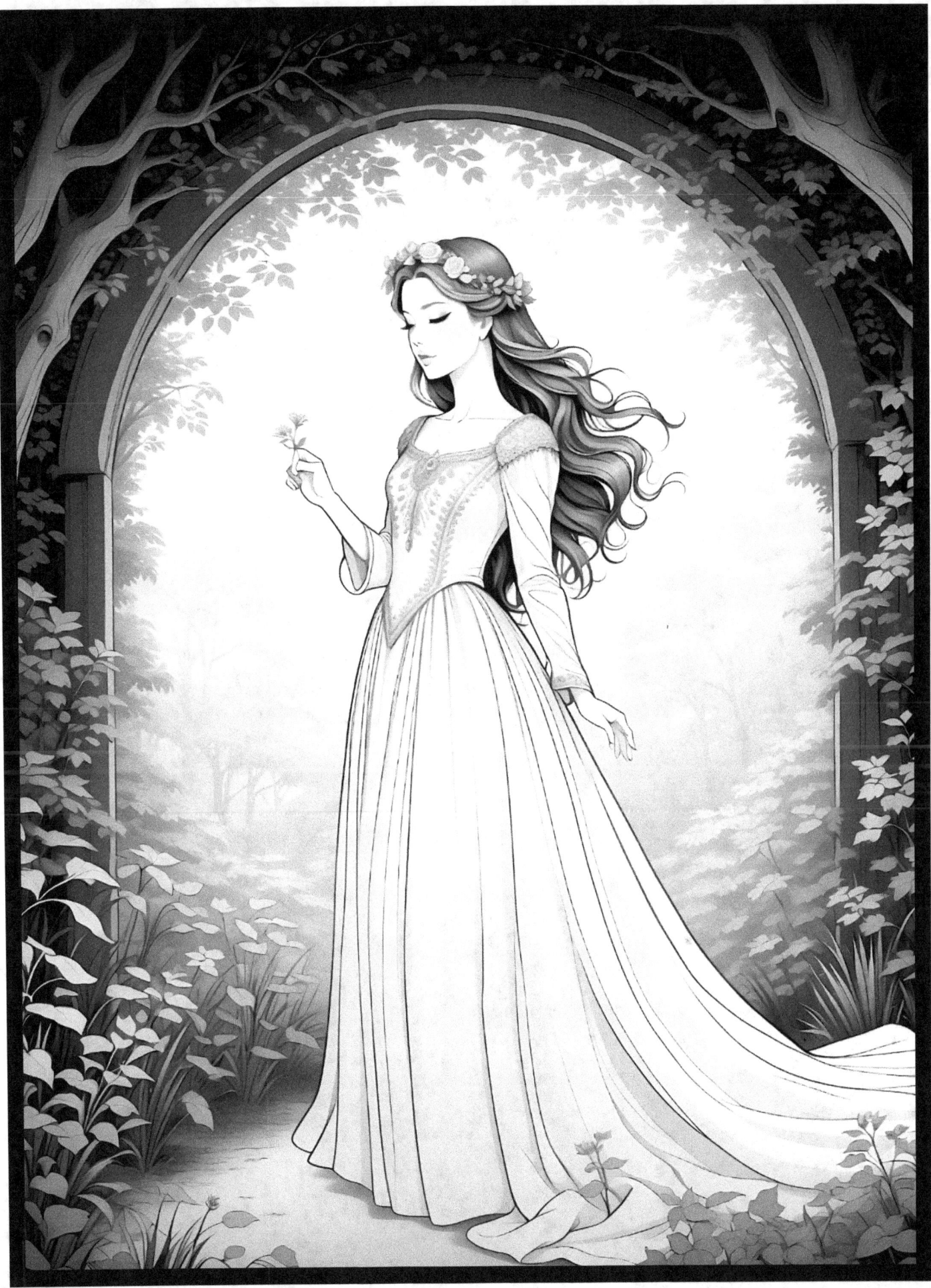

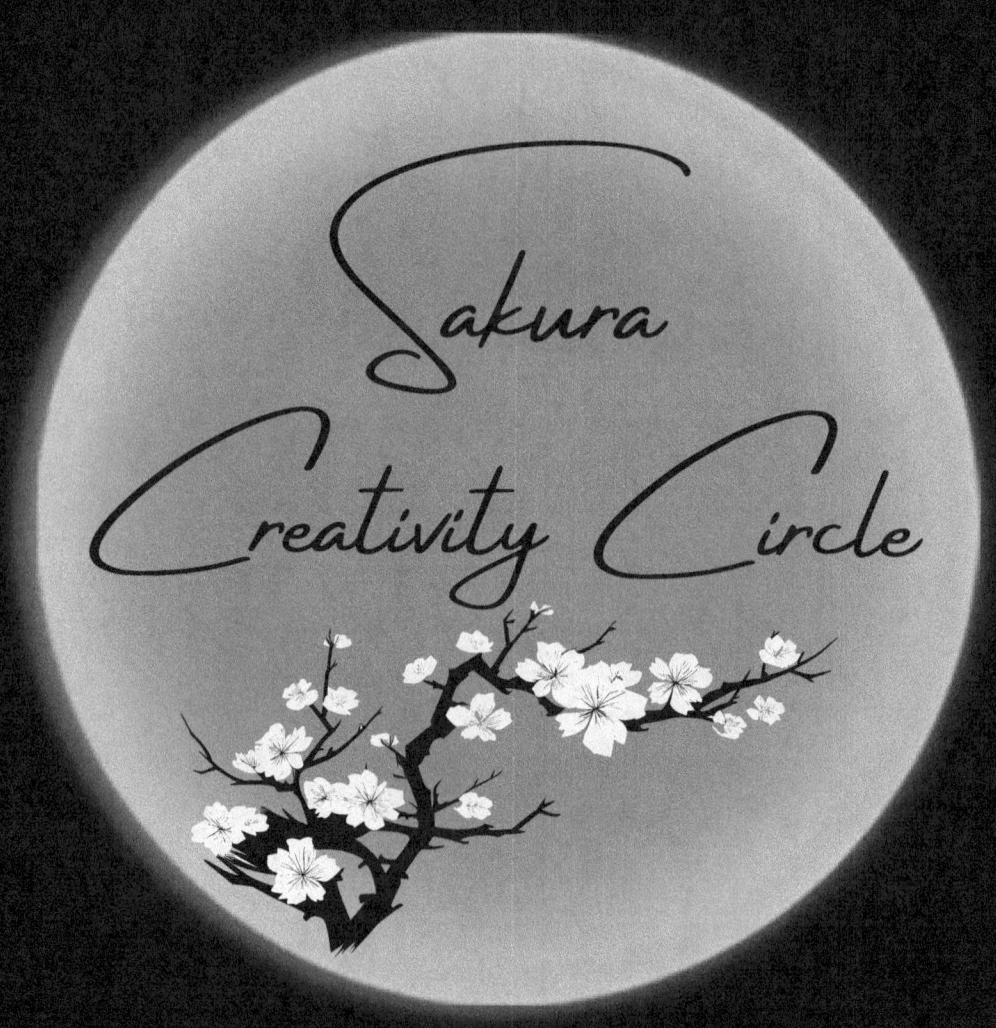

sakuracreativitycircle.com

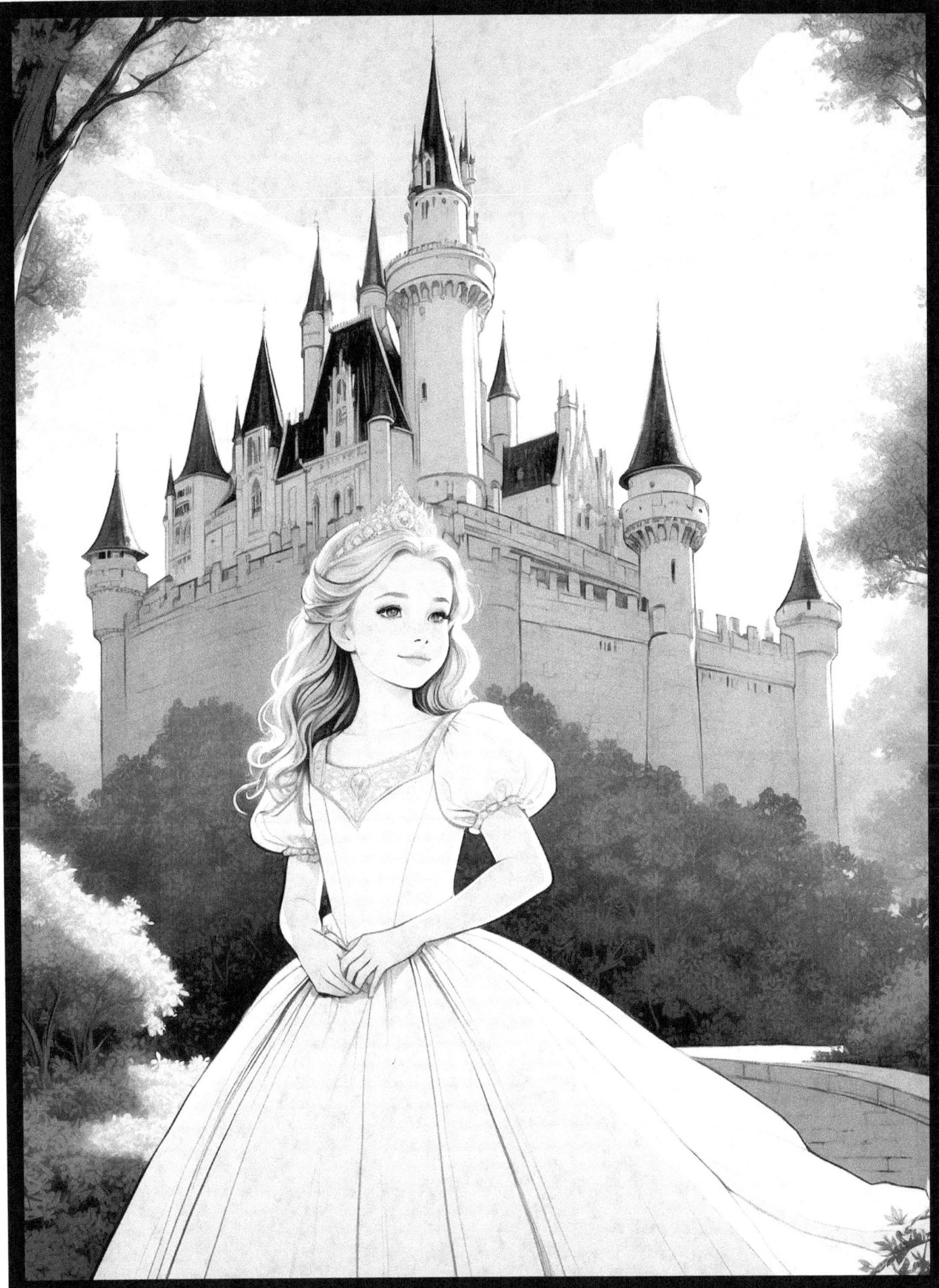

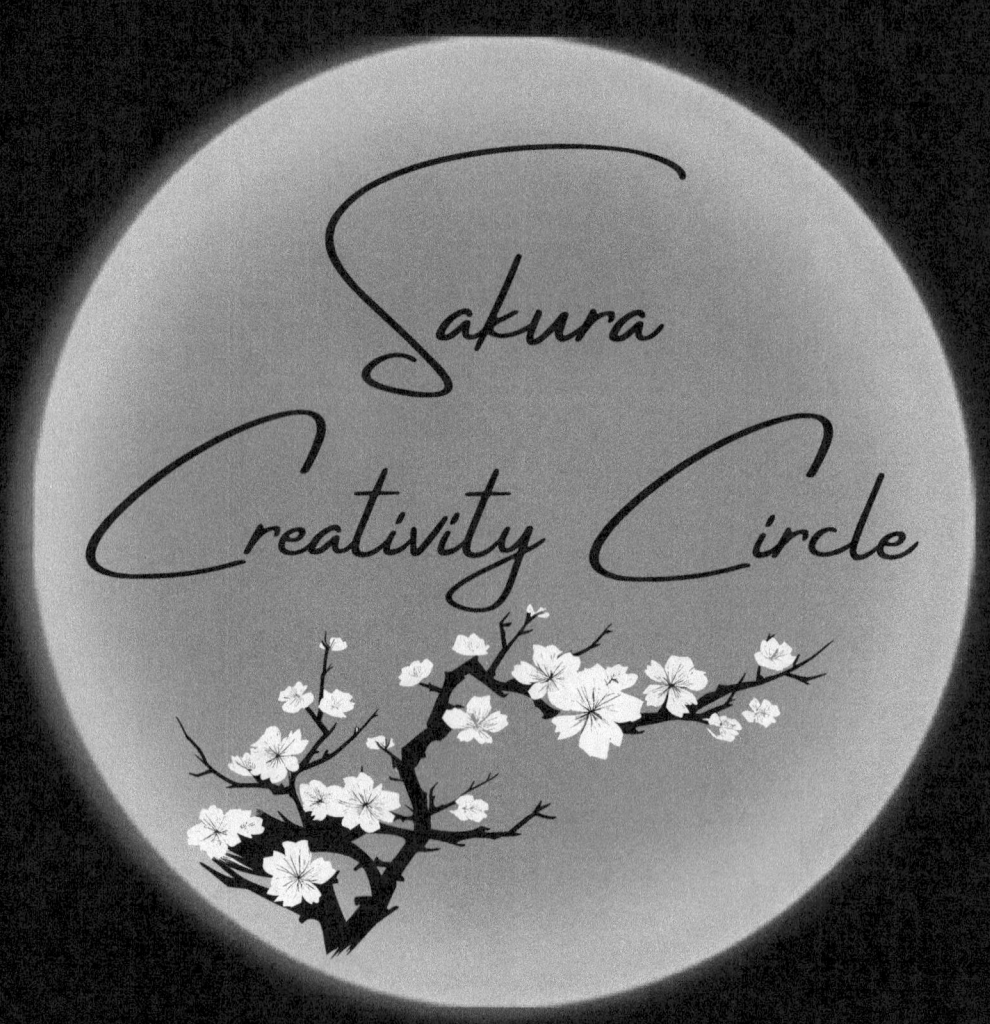

sakuracreativitycircle.com

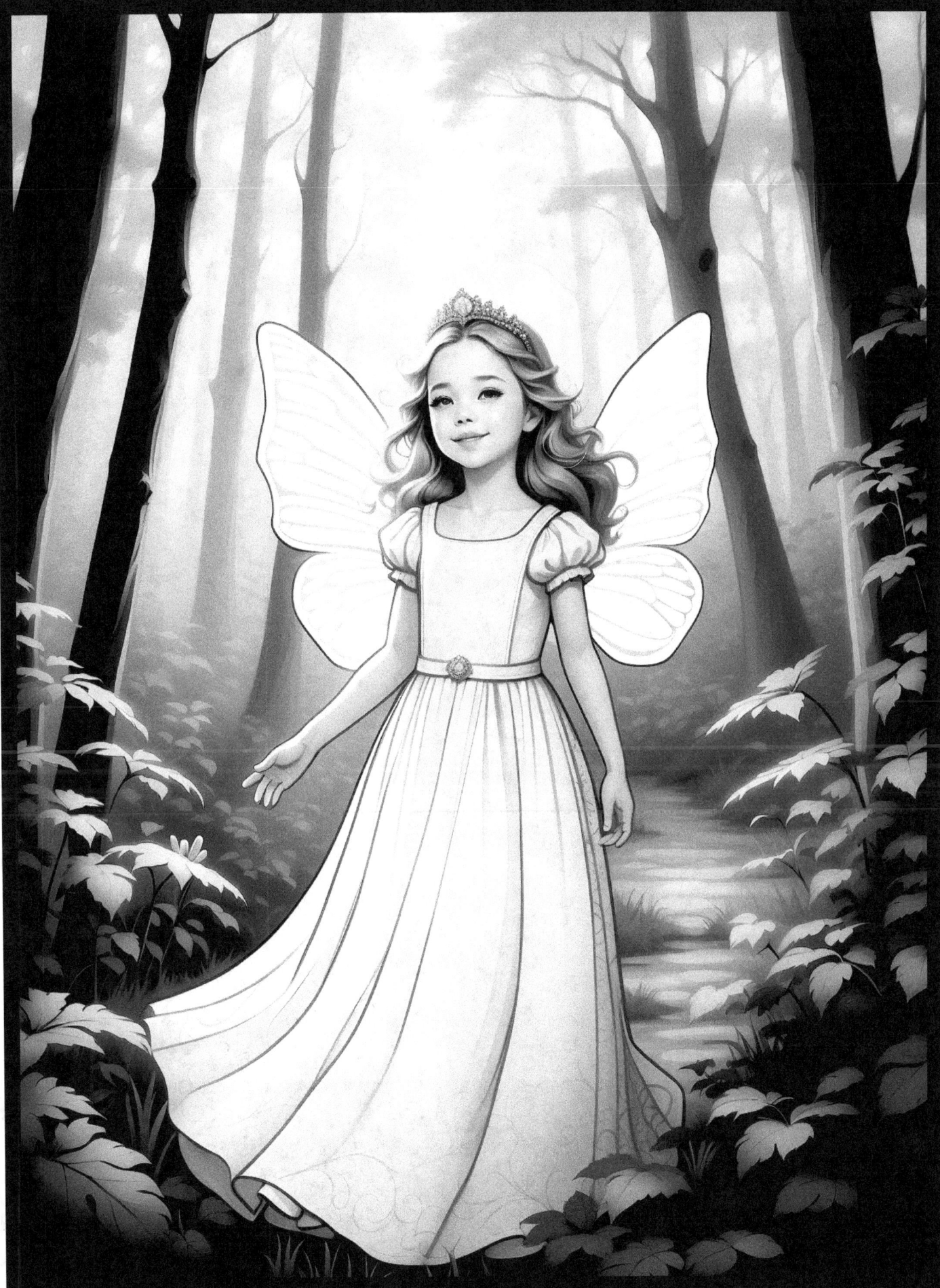

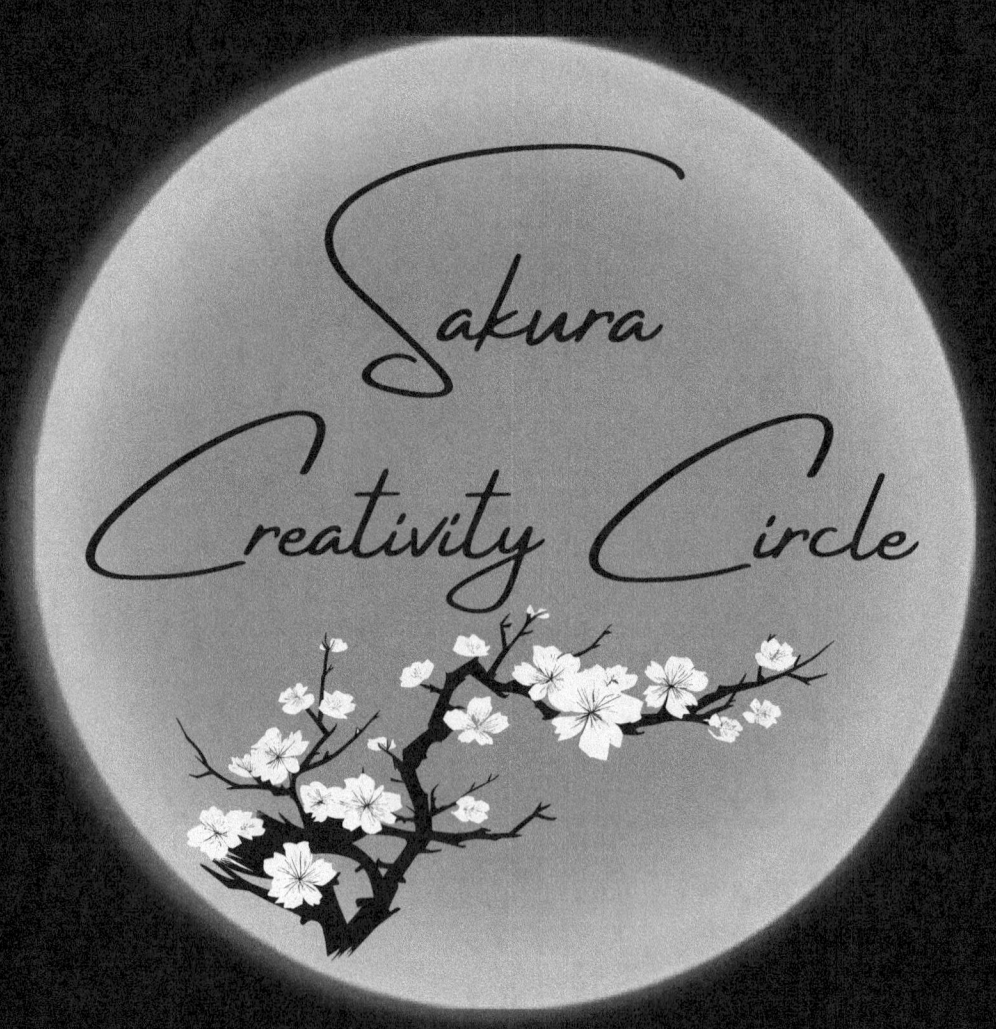

sakuracreativitycircle.com

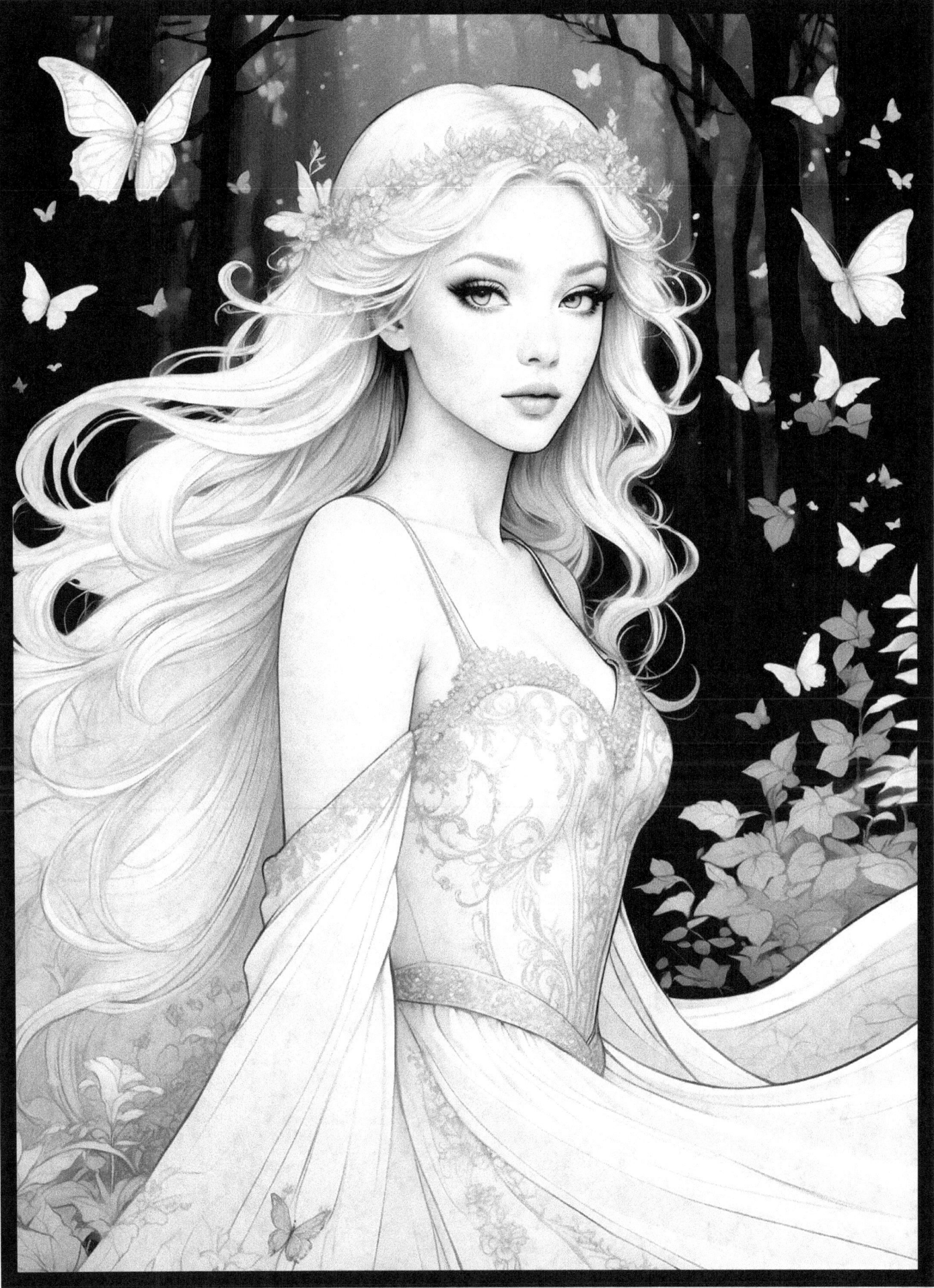

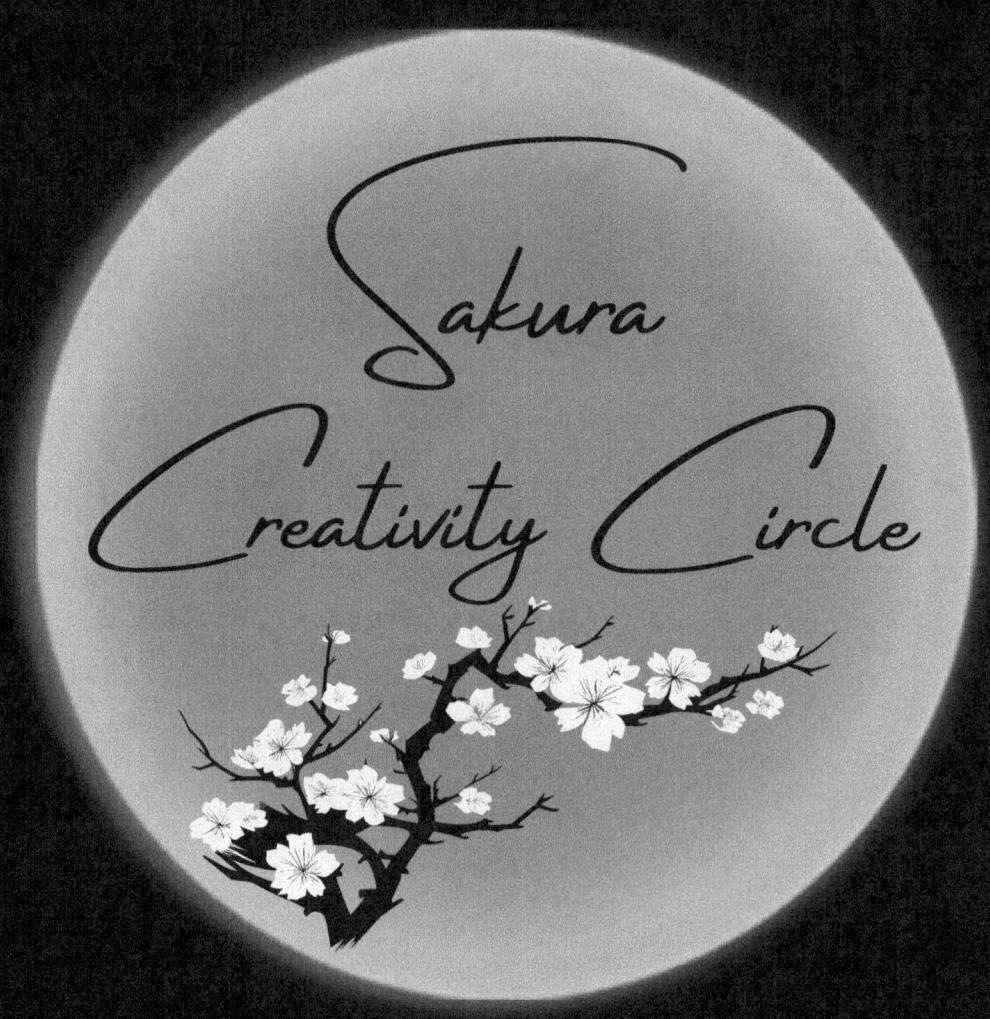

sakuracreativitycircle.com

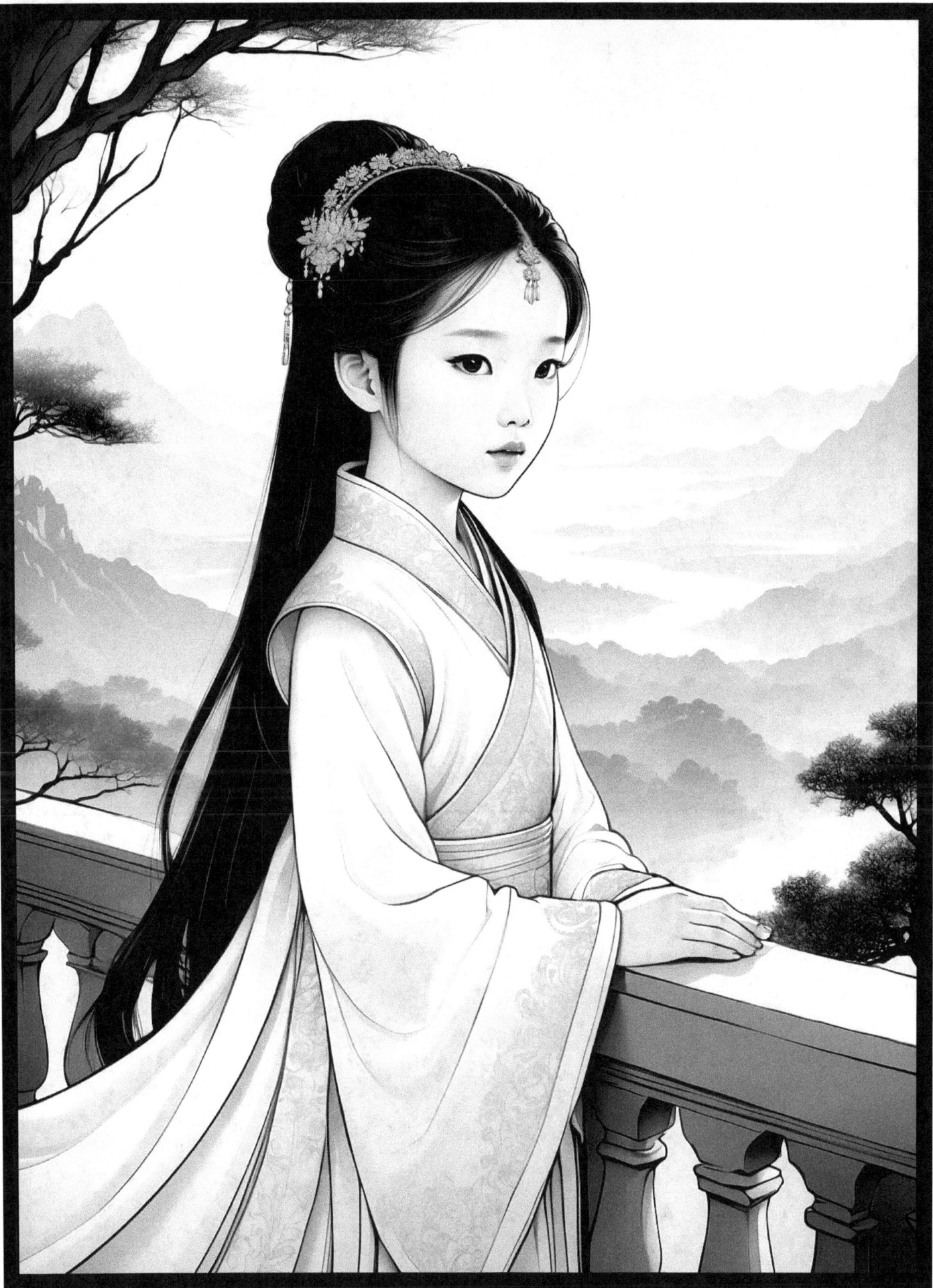

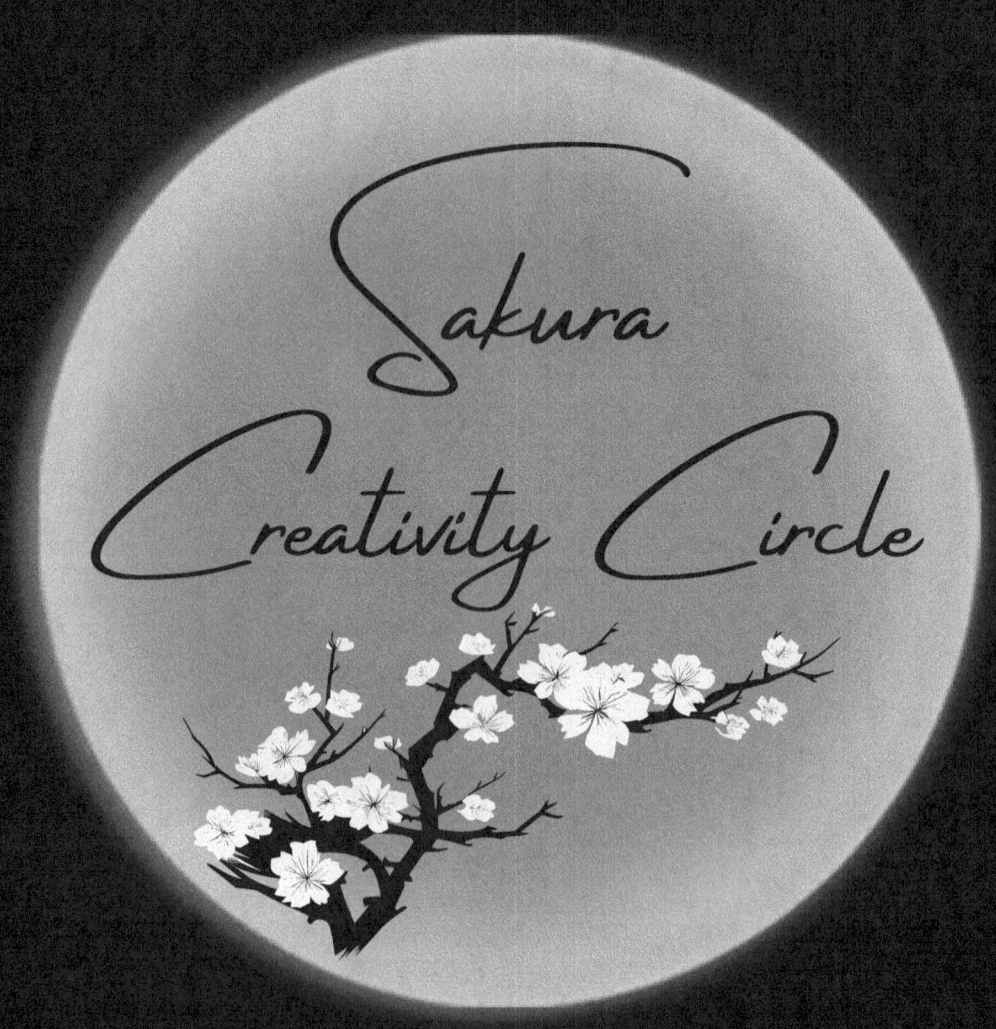

sakuracreativitycircle.com

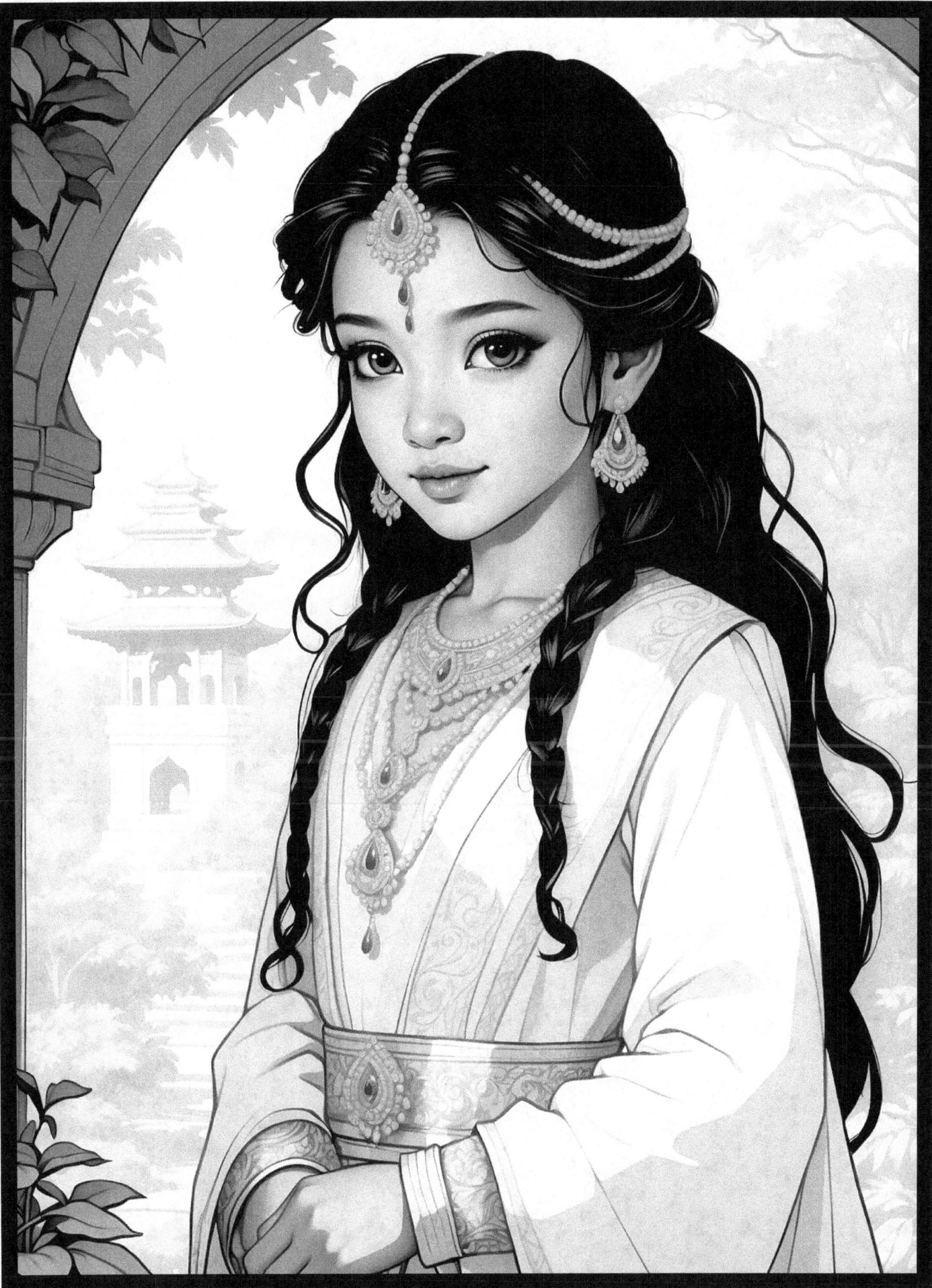

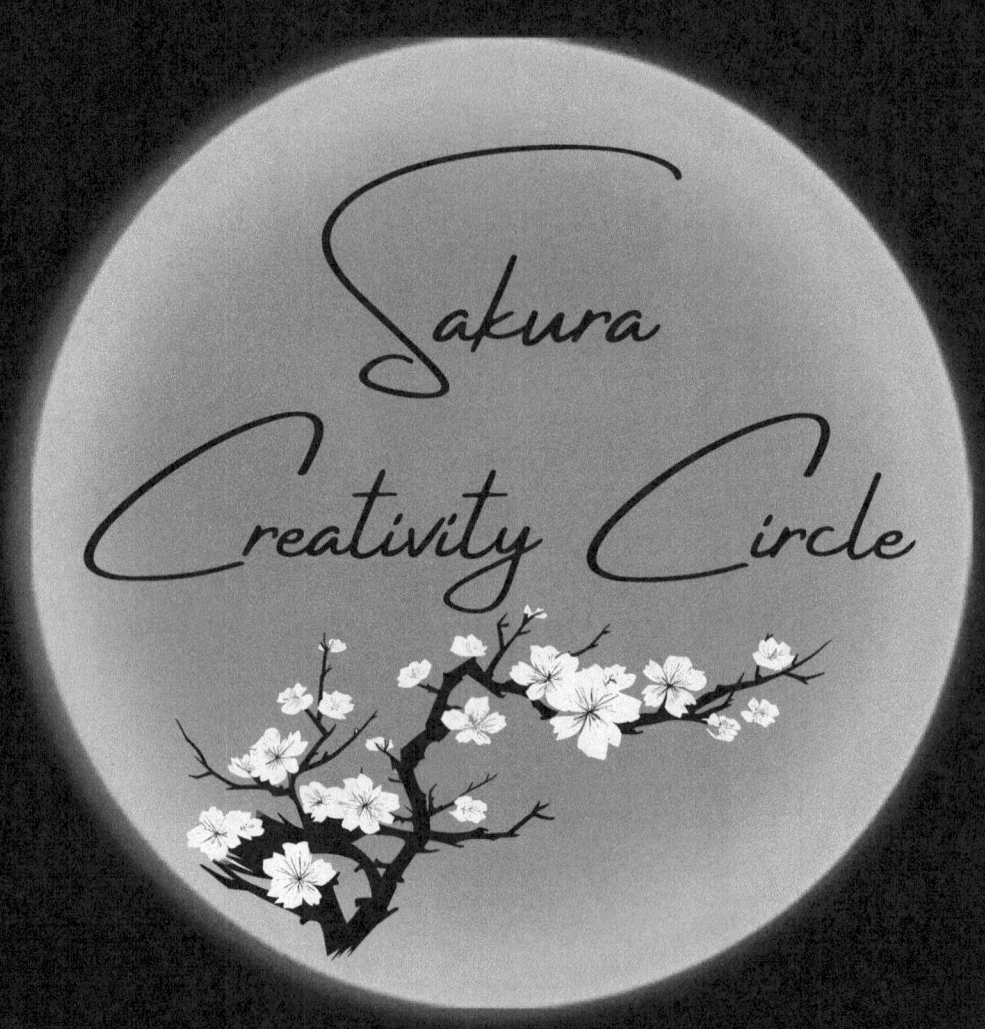

sakuracreativitycircle.com

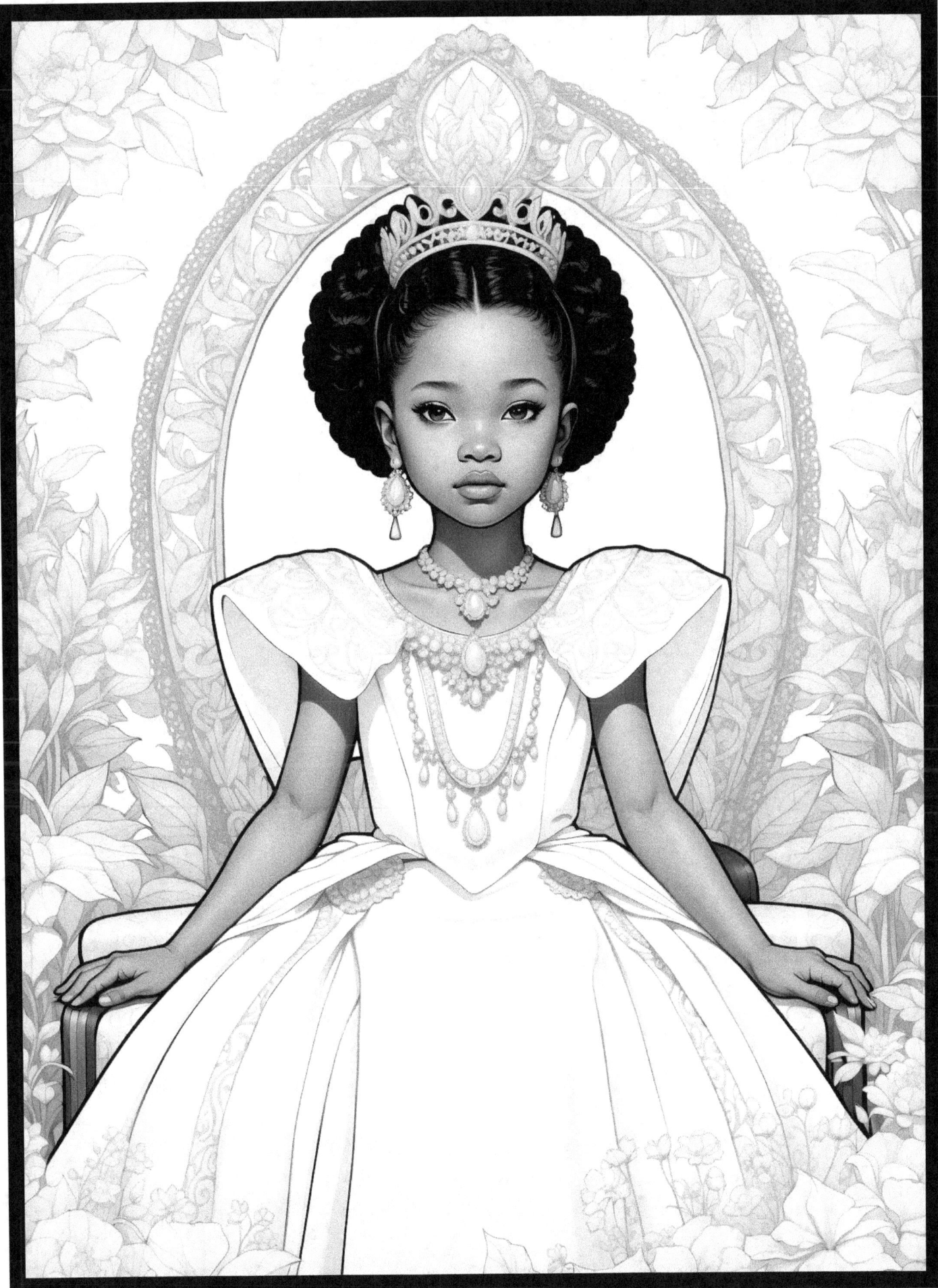

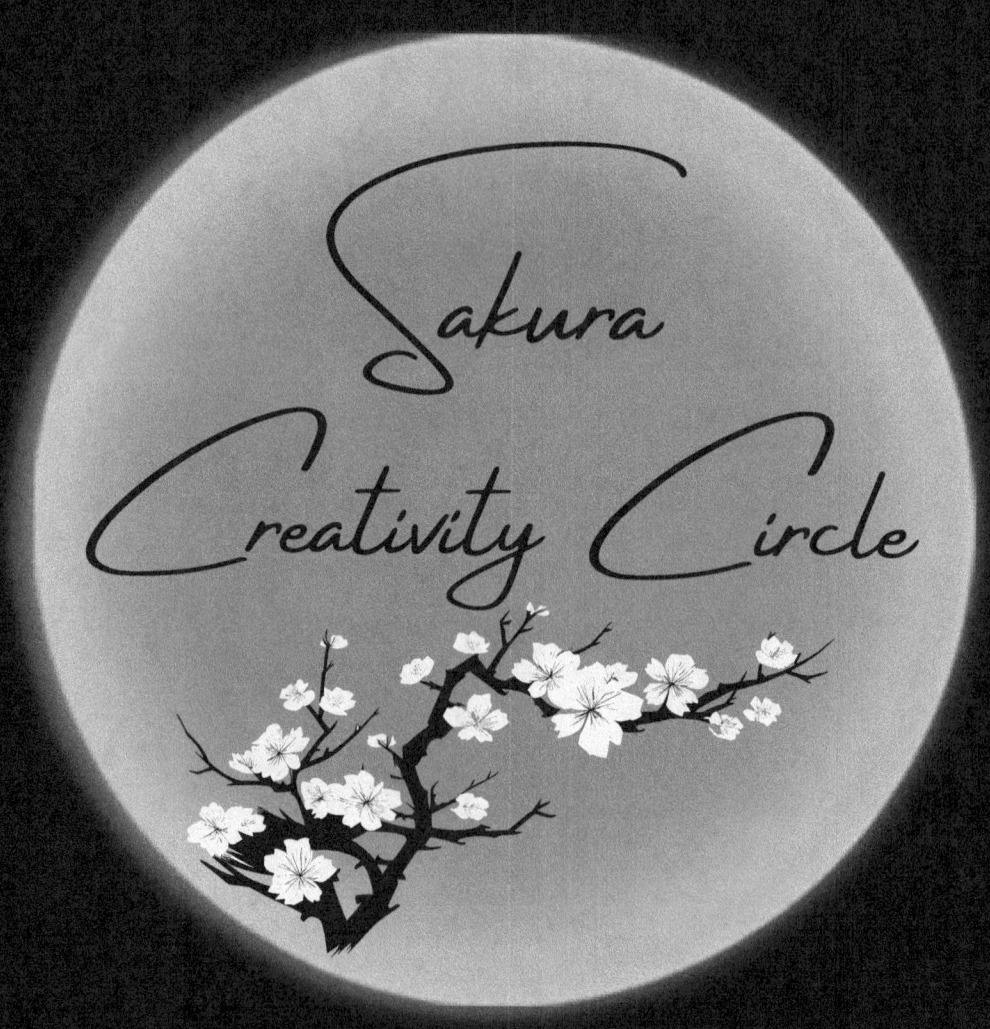

sakuracreativitycircle.com

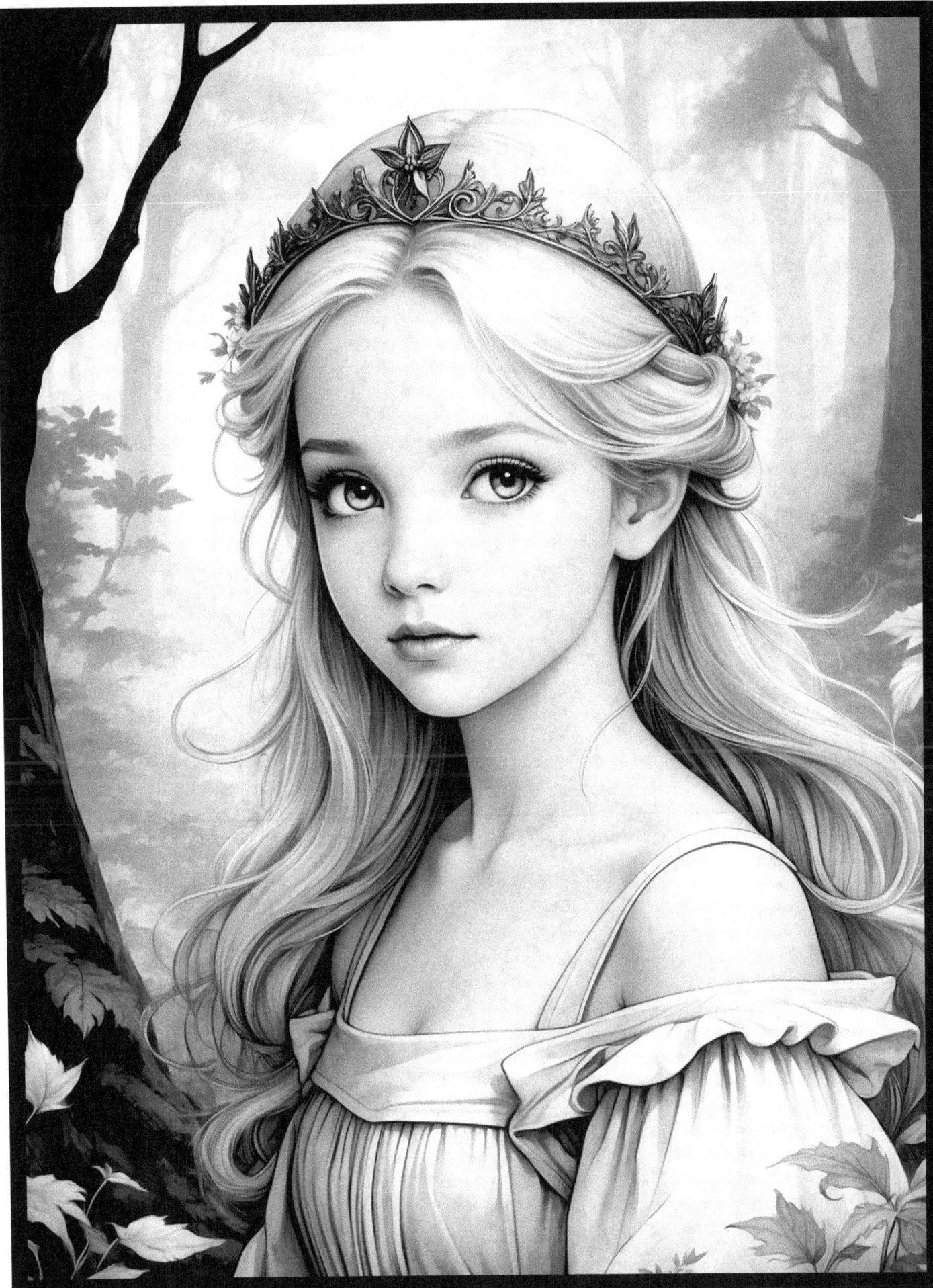

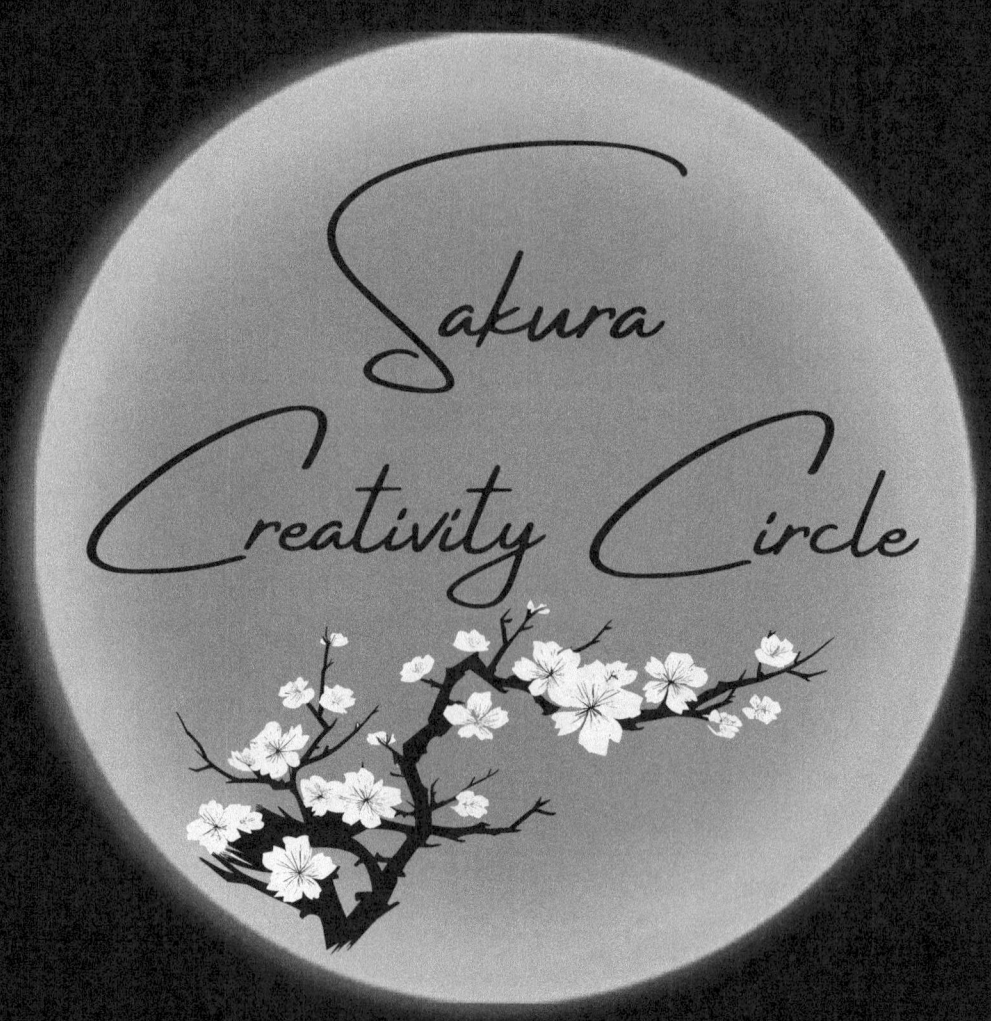

sakuracreativitycircle.com

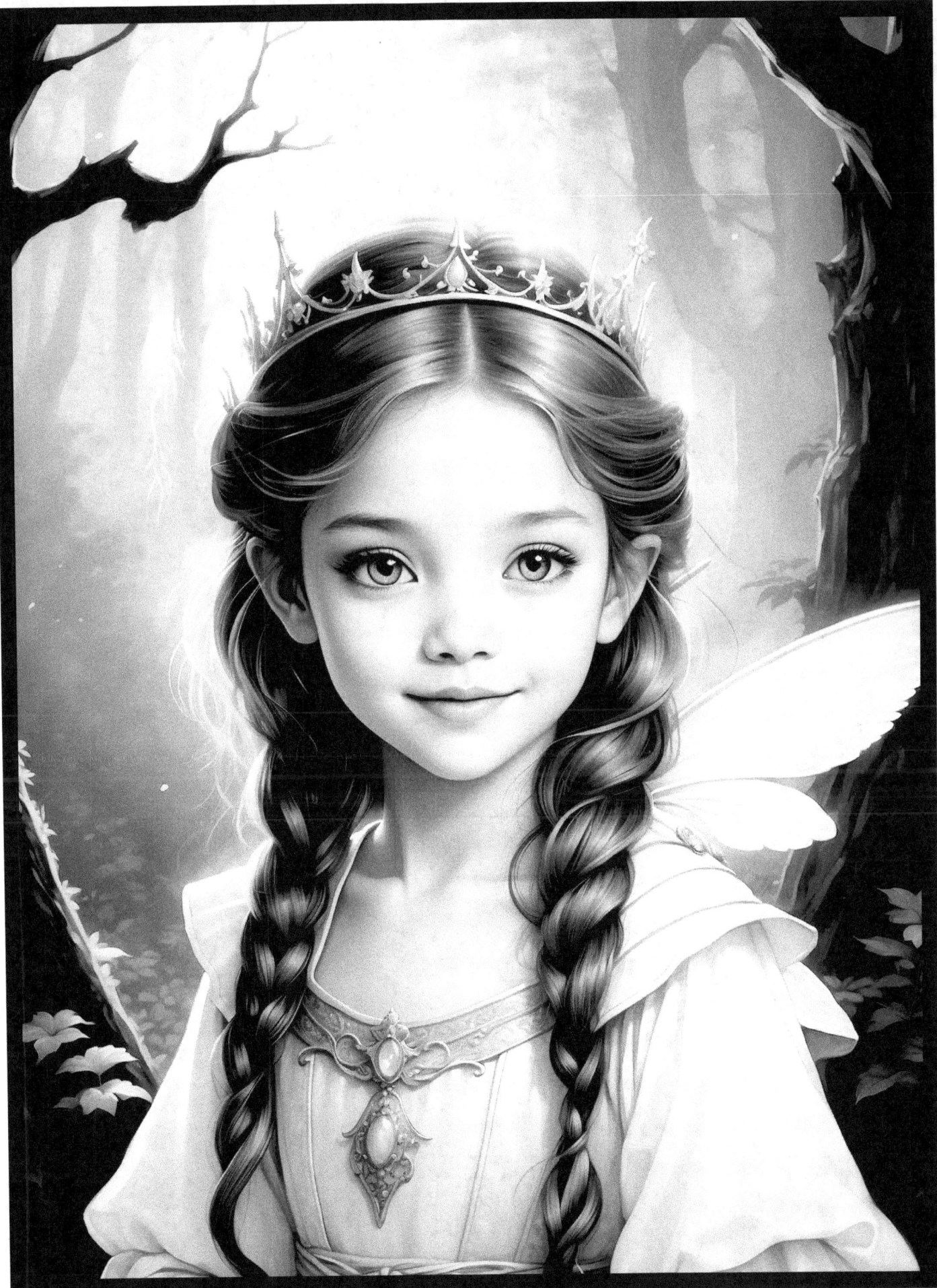

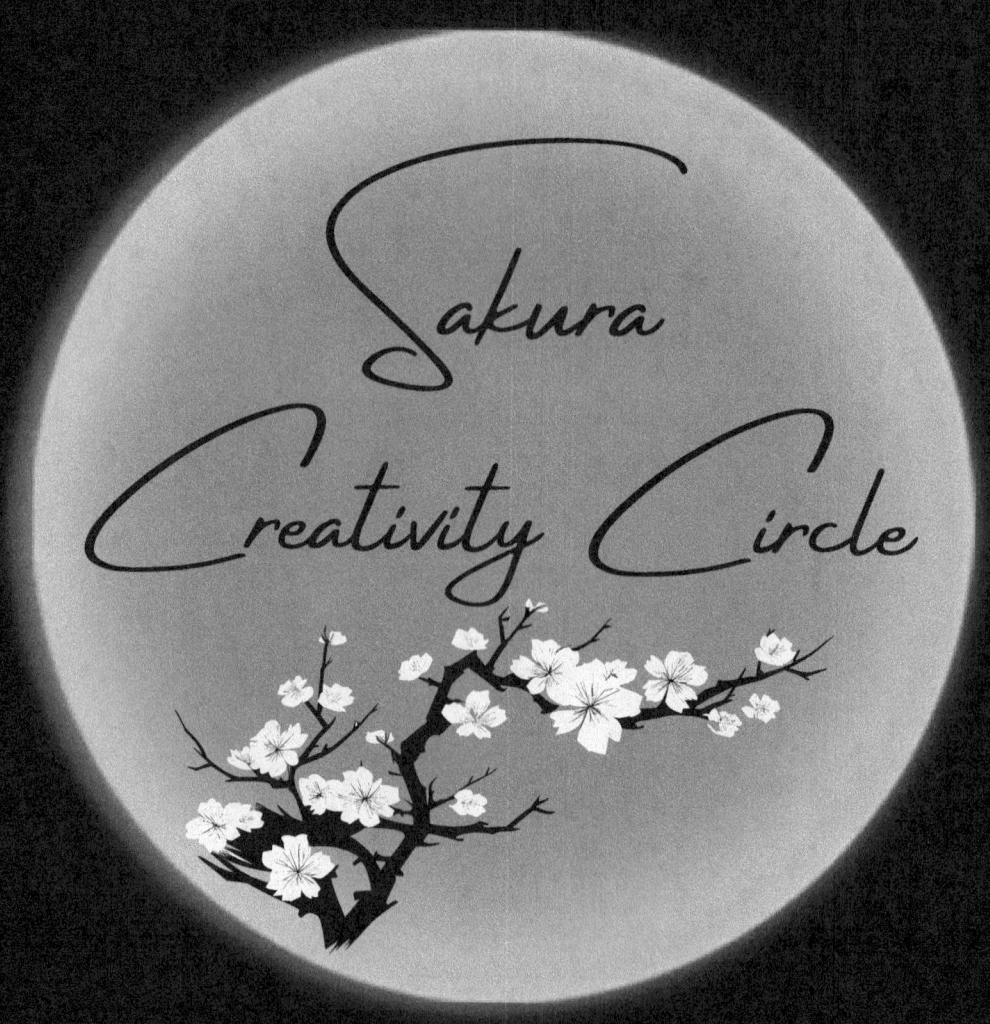

sakuracreativitycircle.com

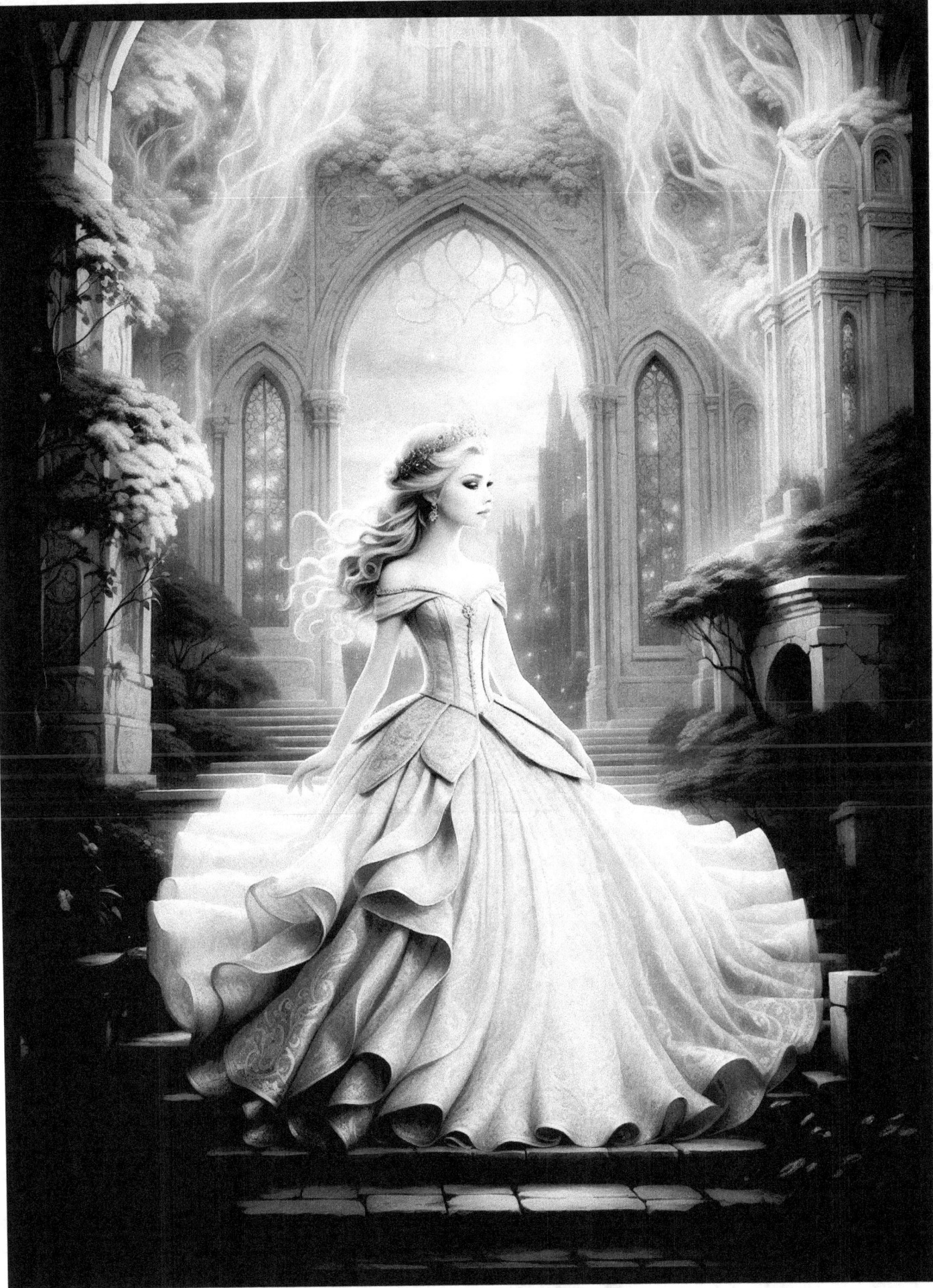

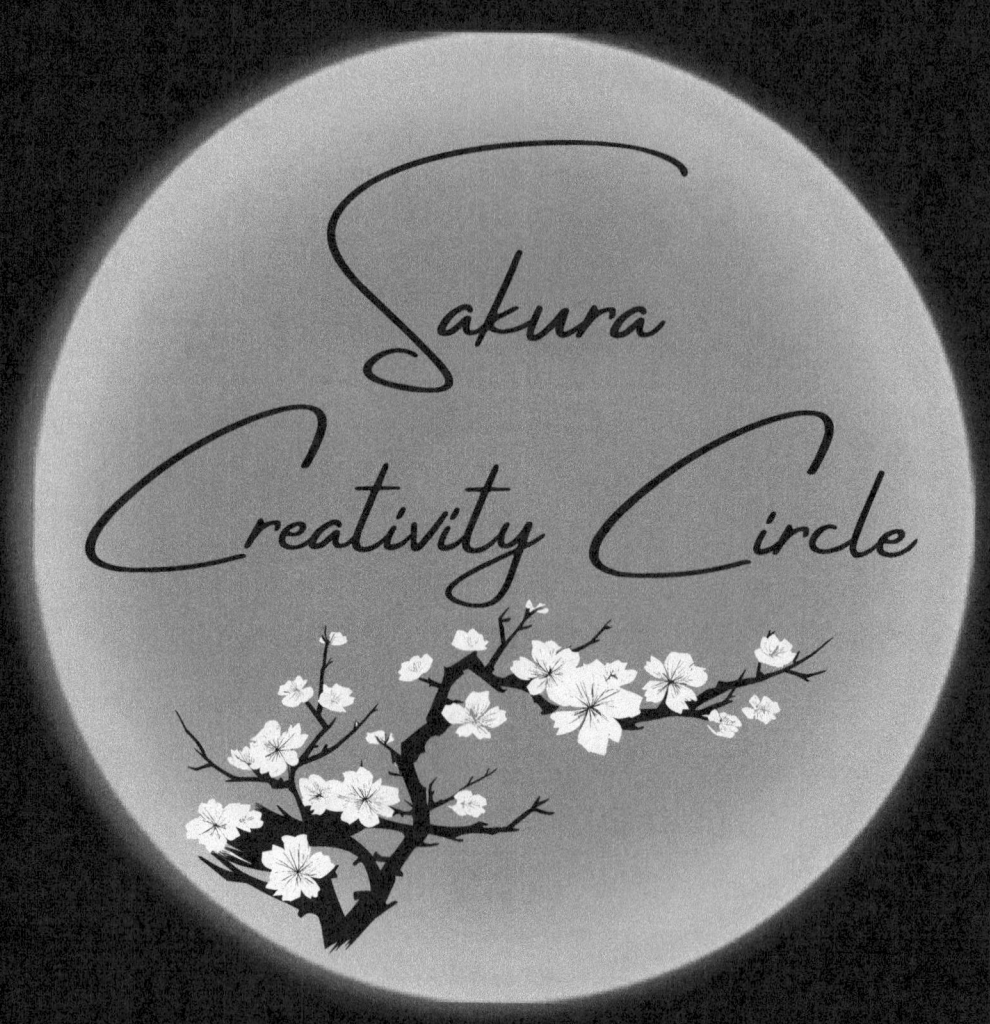

sakuracreativitycircle.com

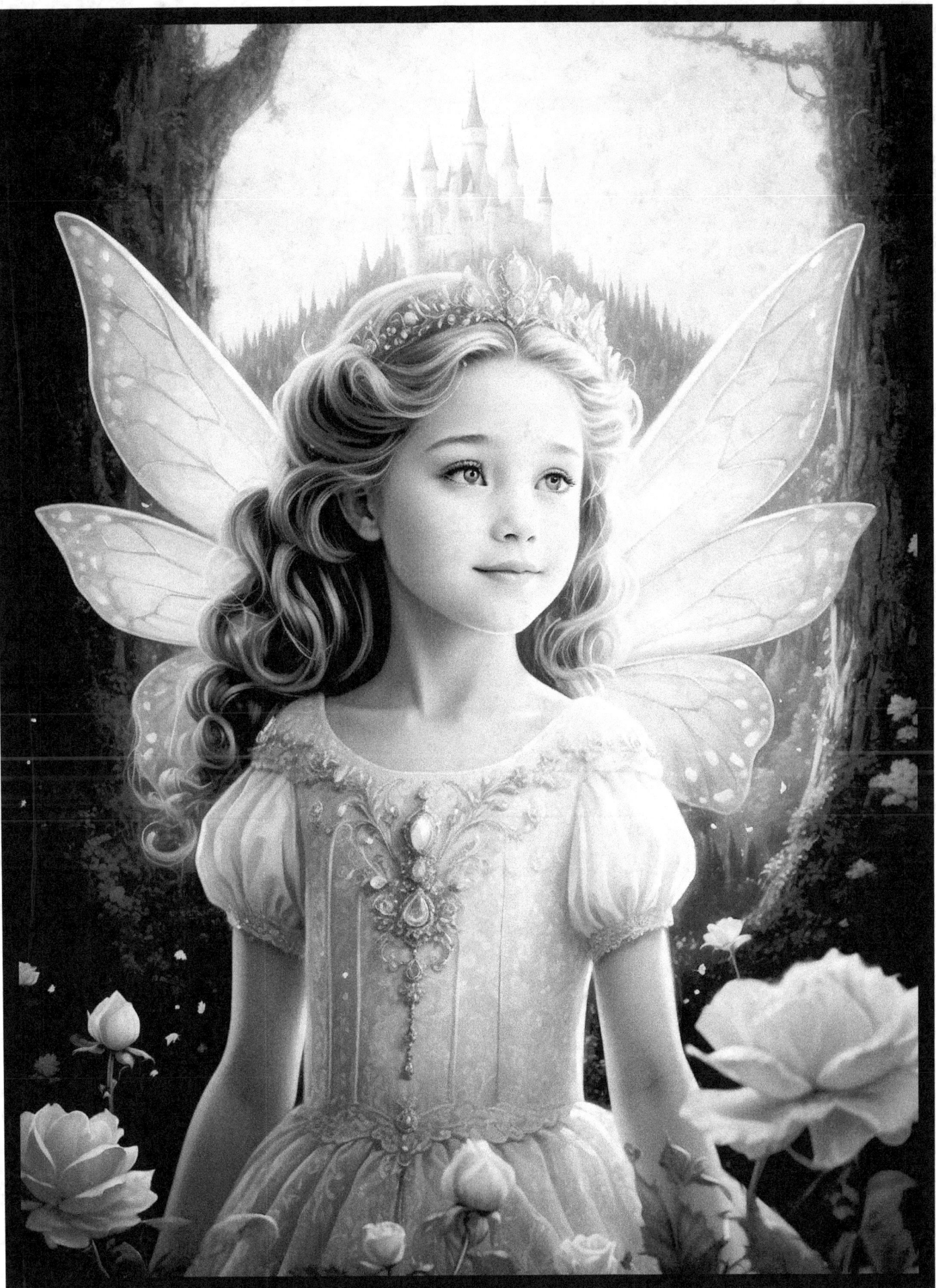

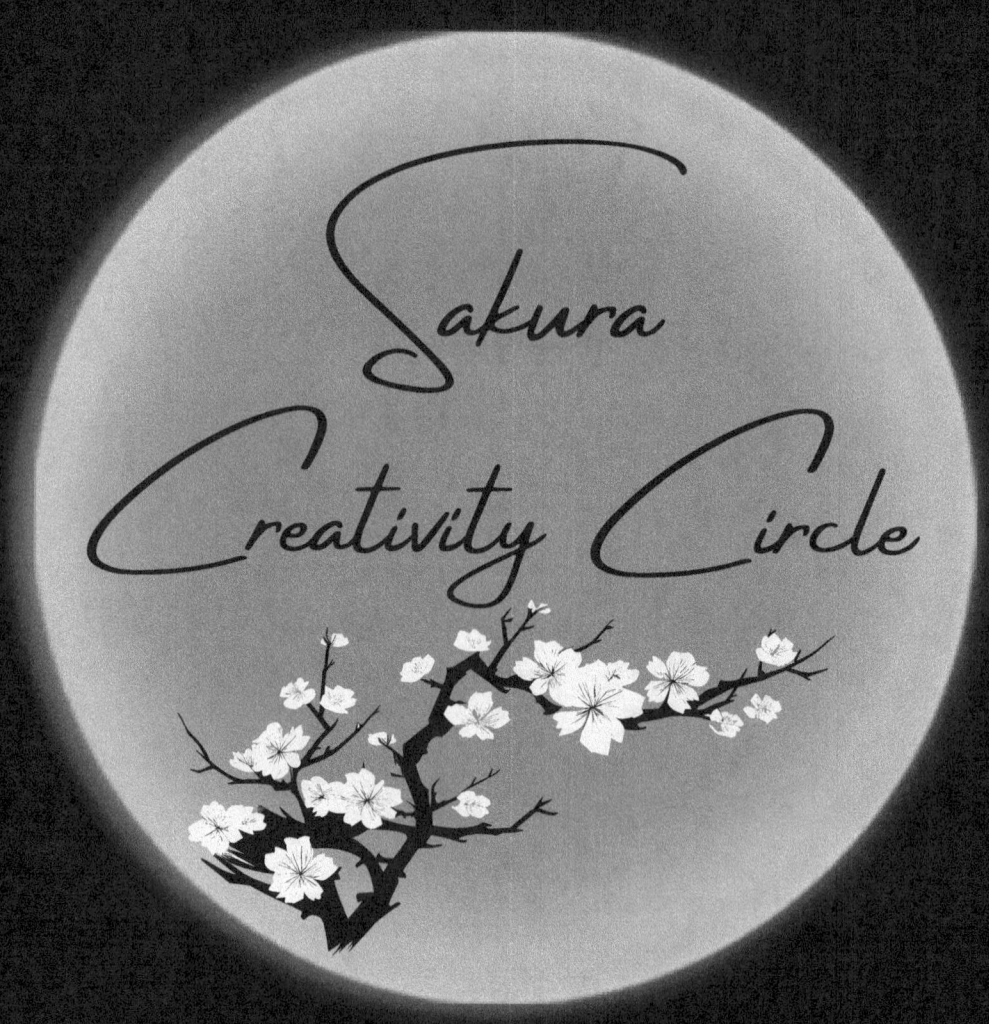

sakuracreativitycircle.com

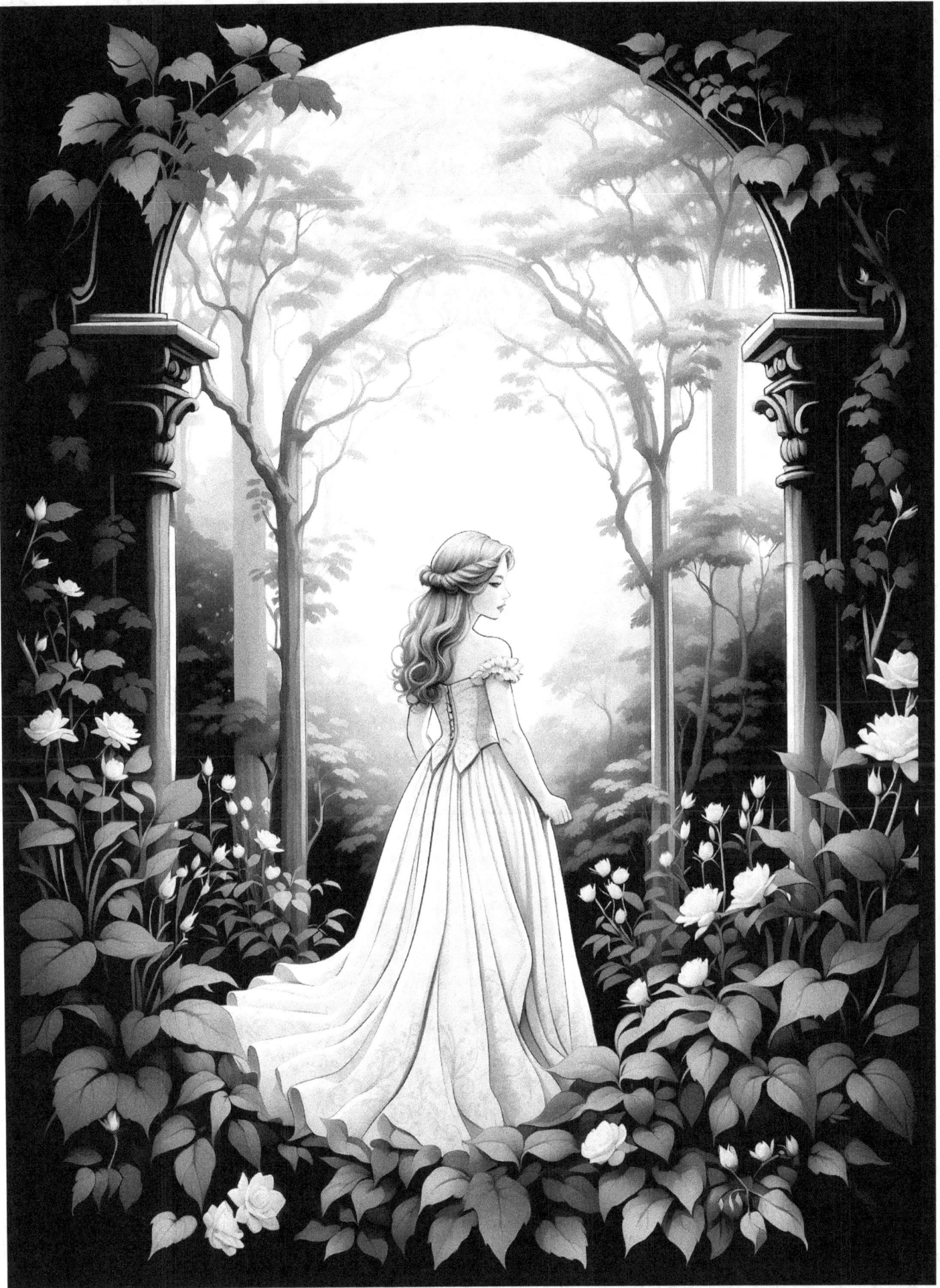

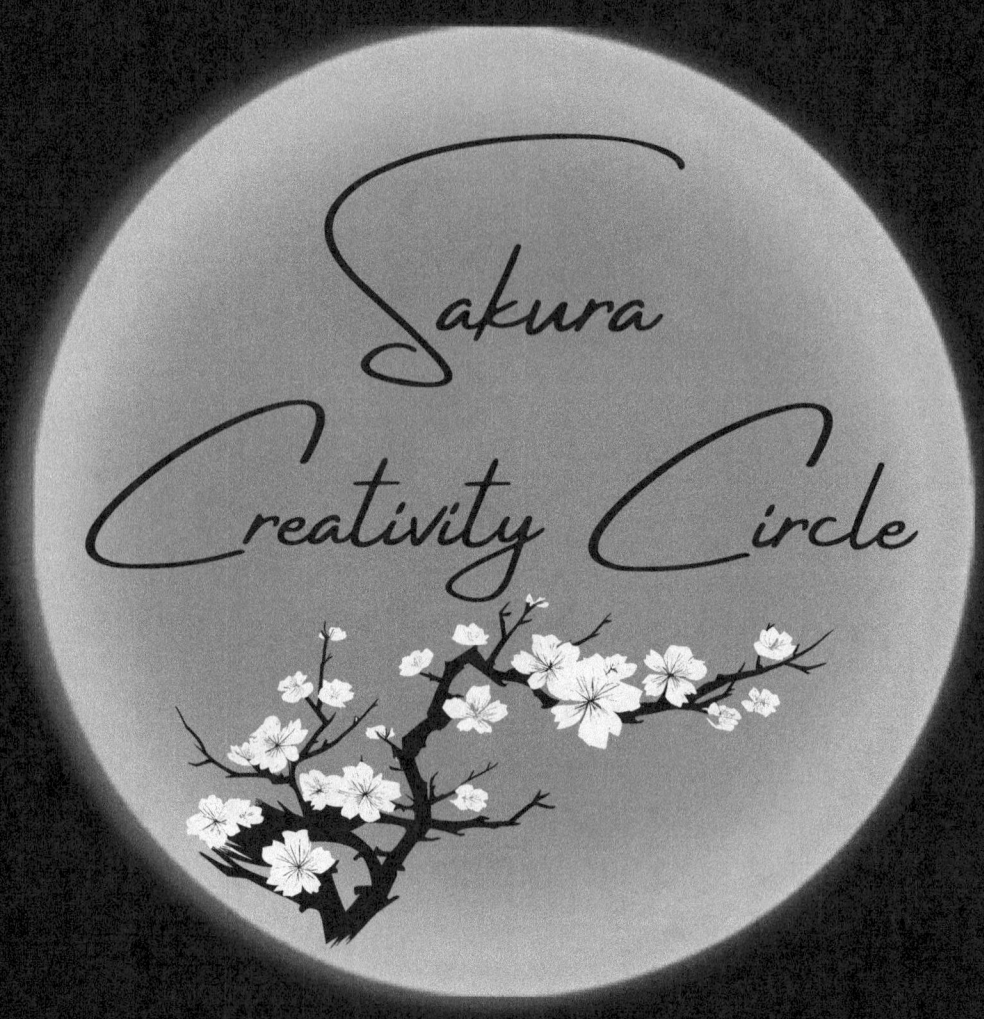

sakuracreativitycircle.com

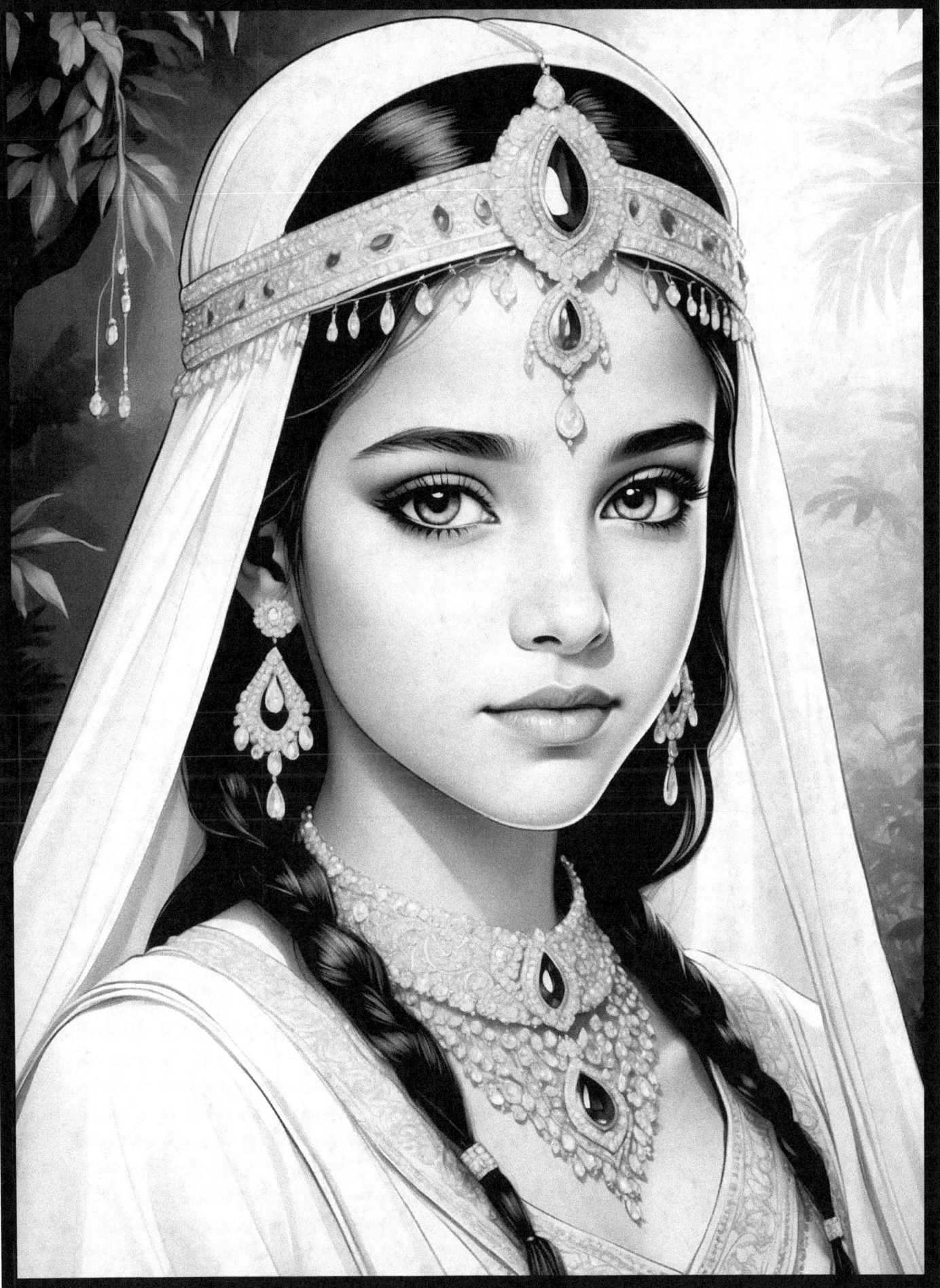

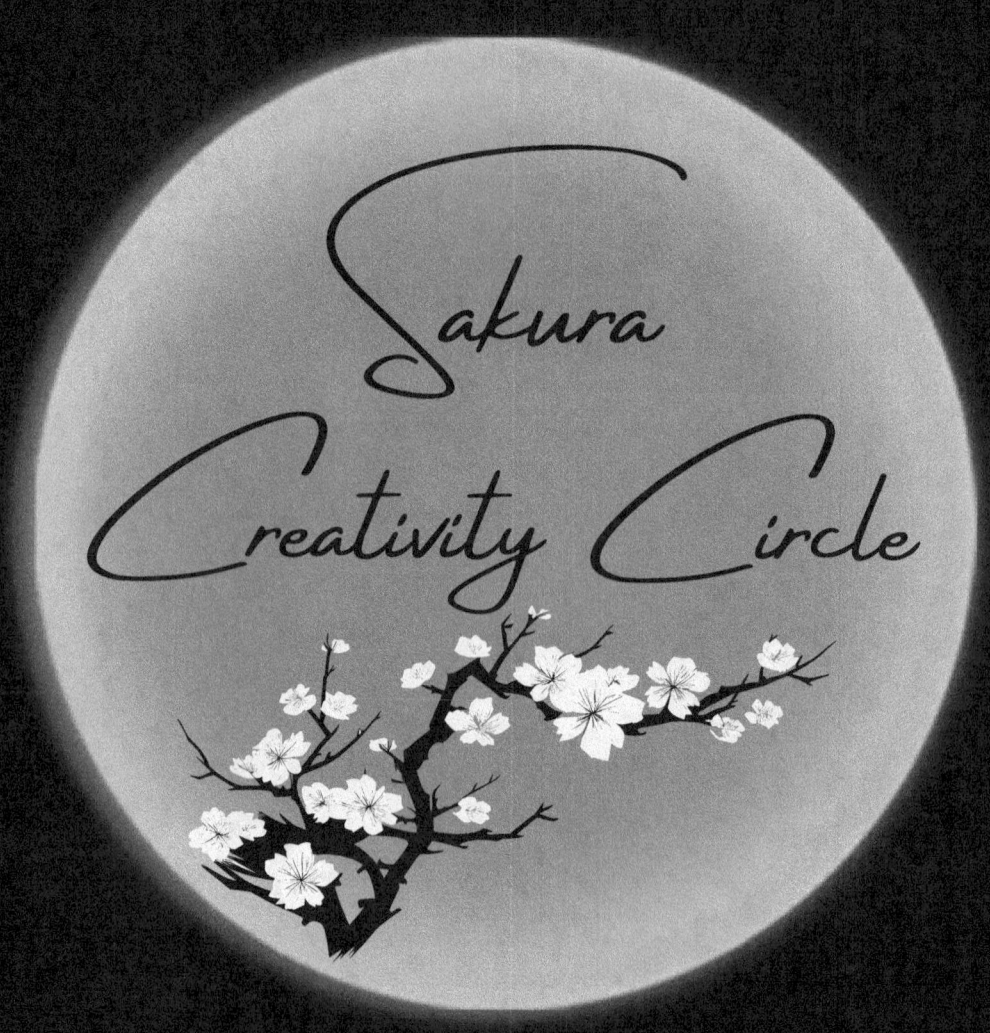

sakuracreativitycircle.com

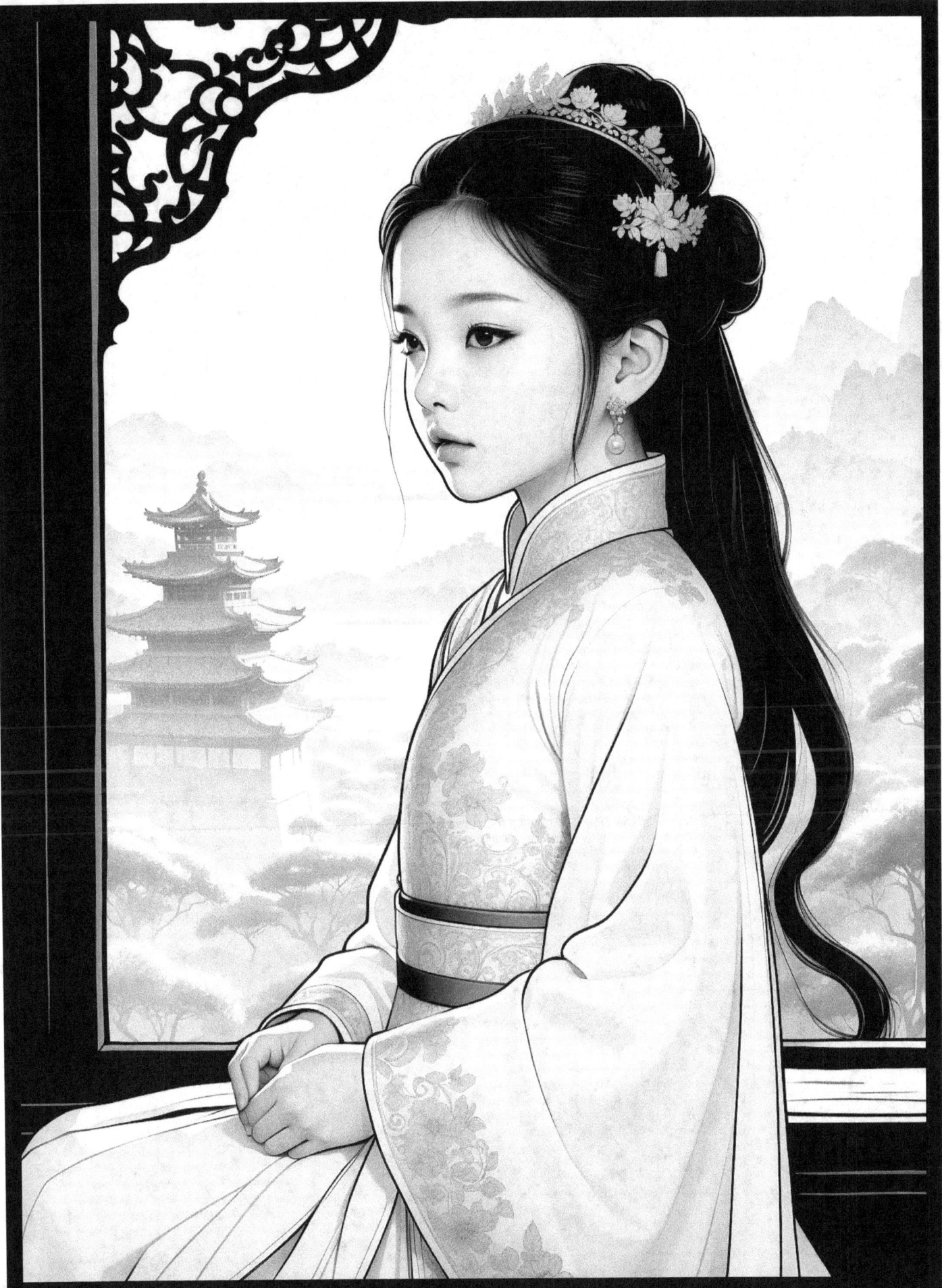

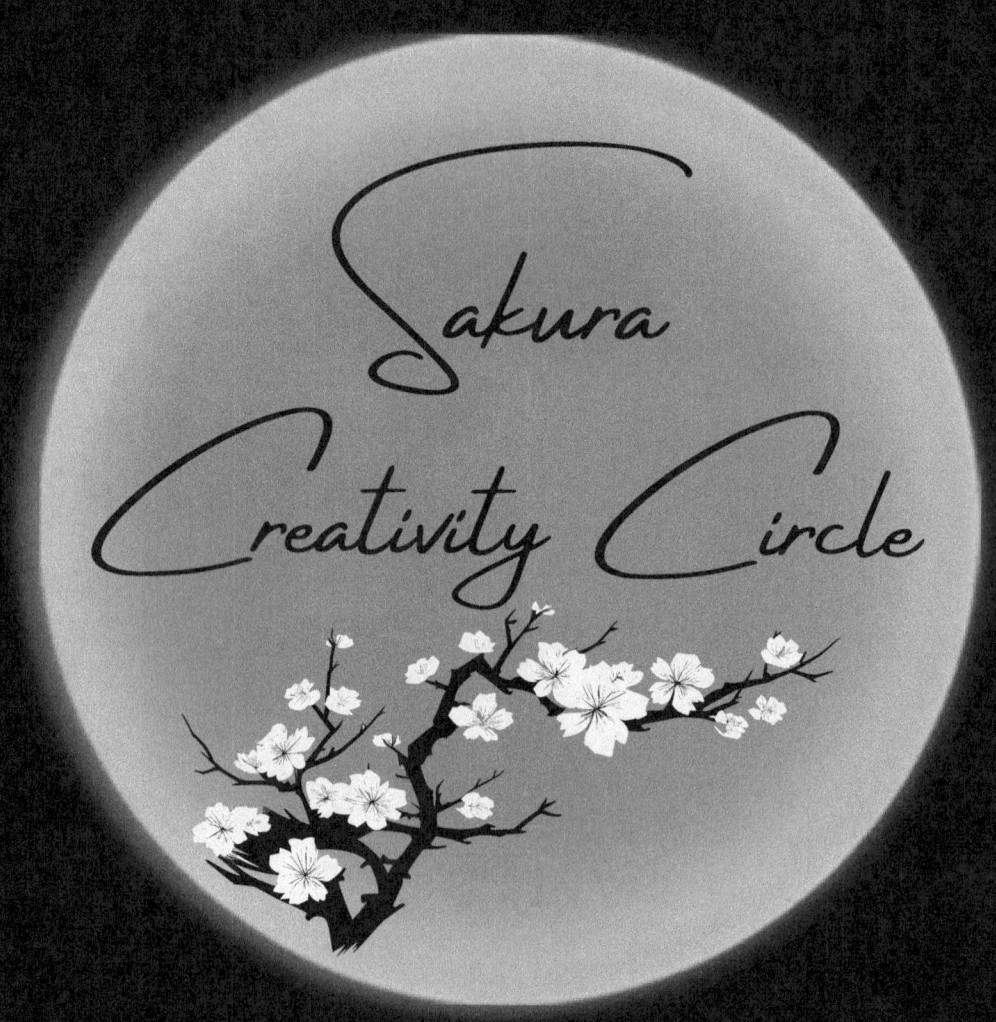

sakuracreativitycircle.com

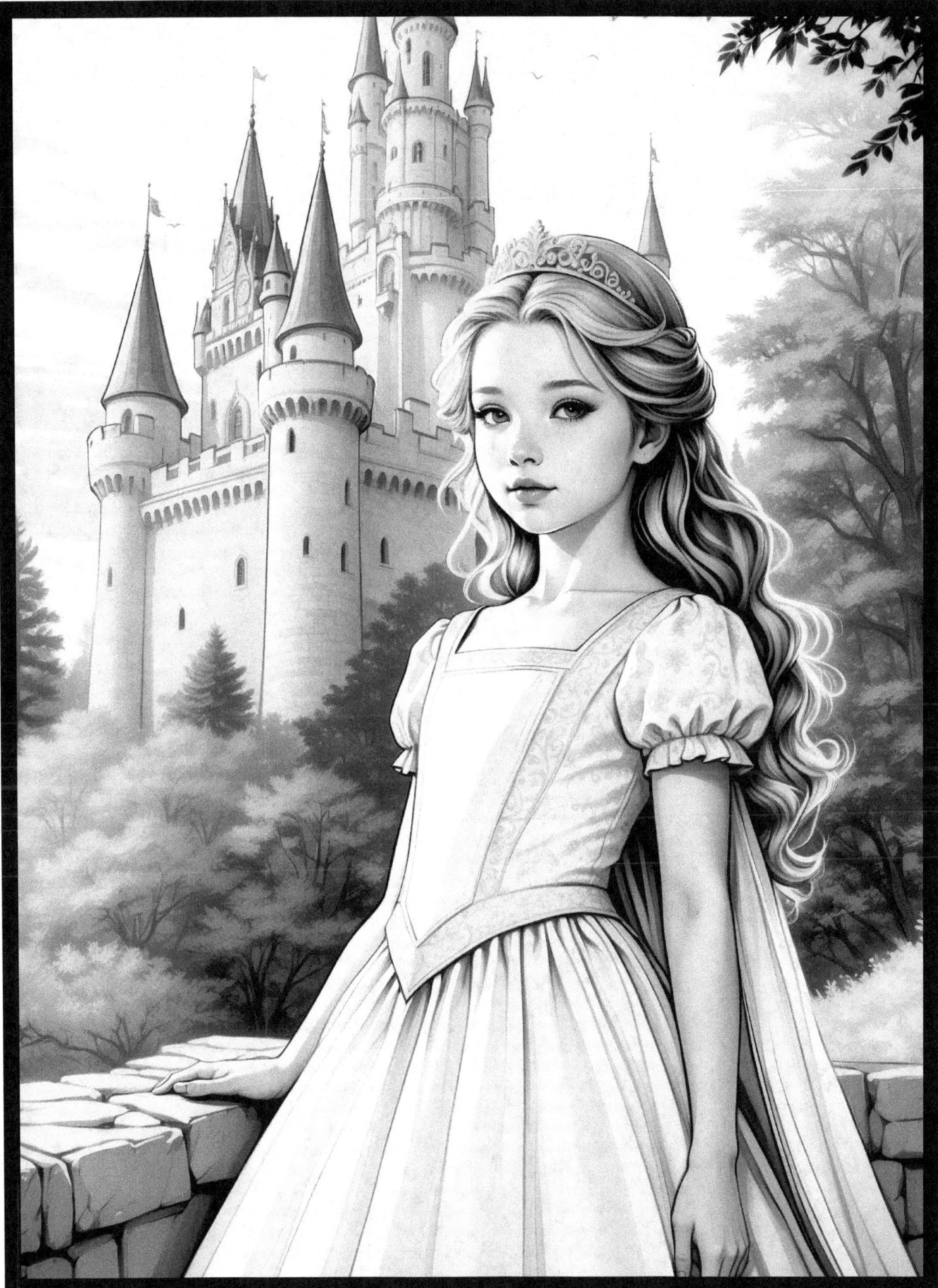

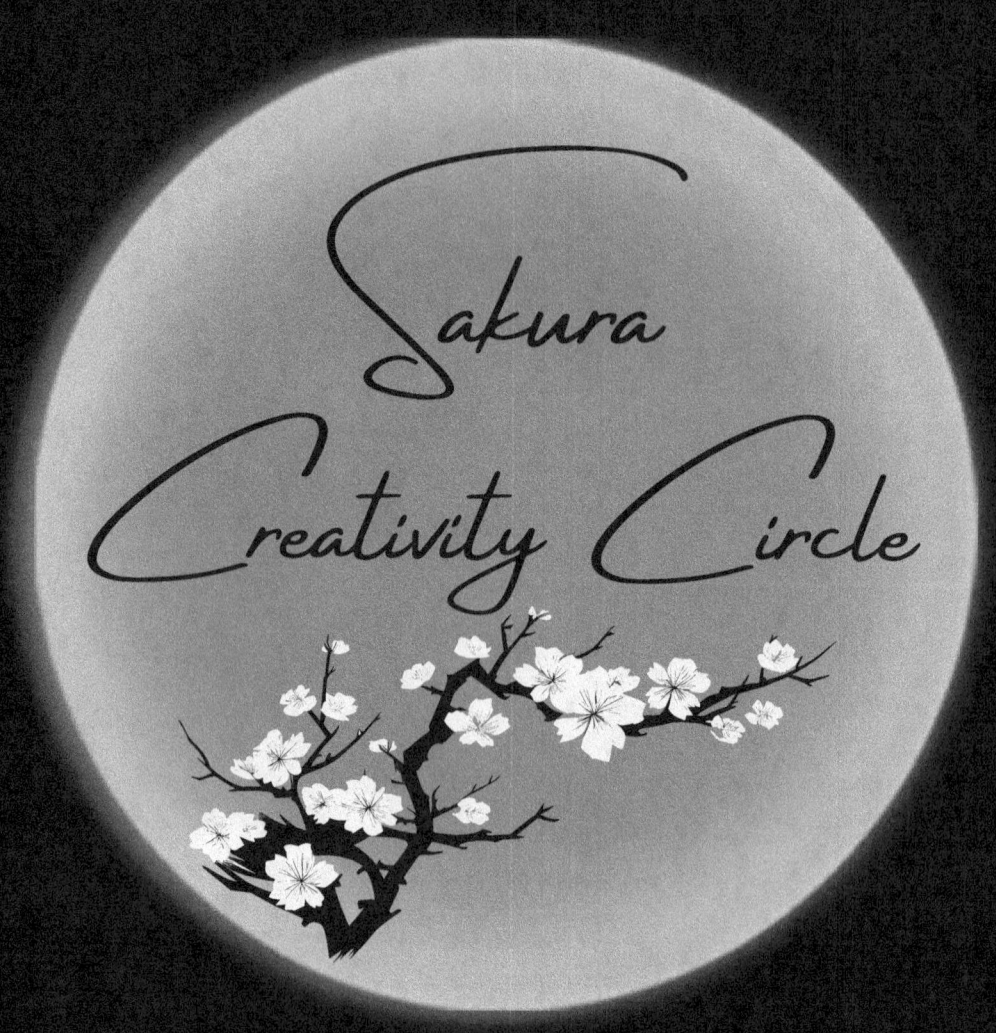

sakuracreativitycircle.com

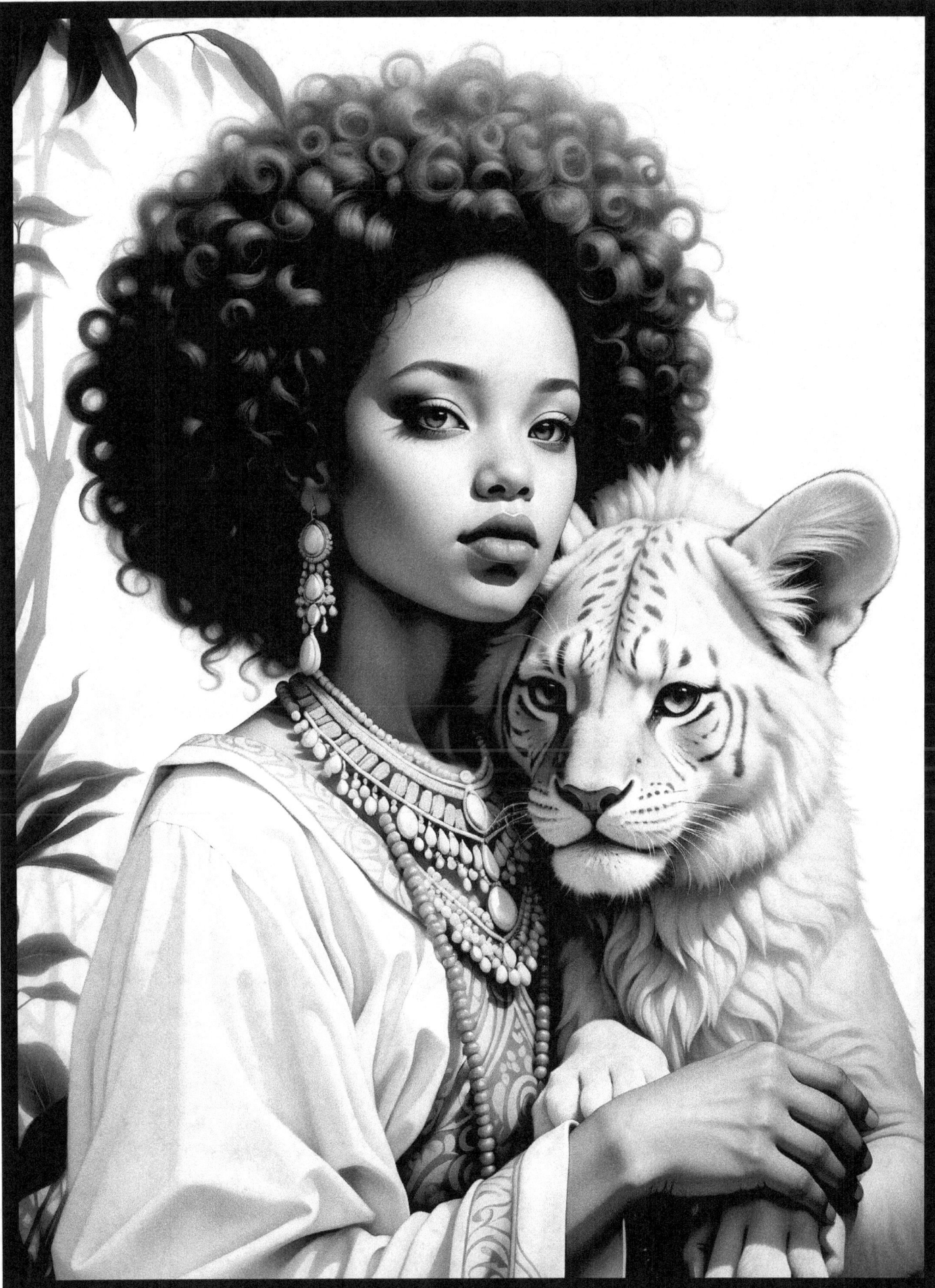

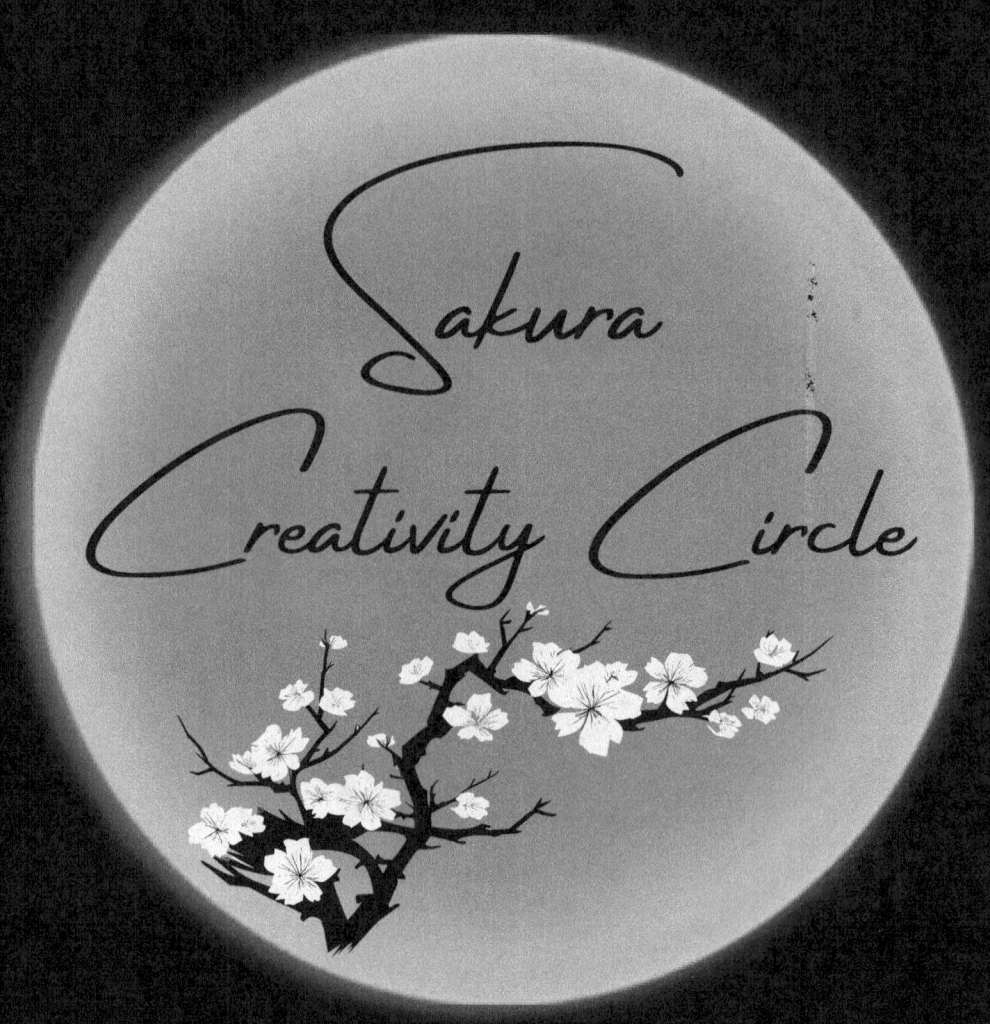

sakuracreativitycircle.com

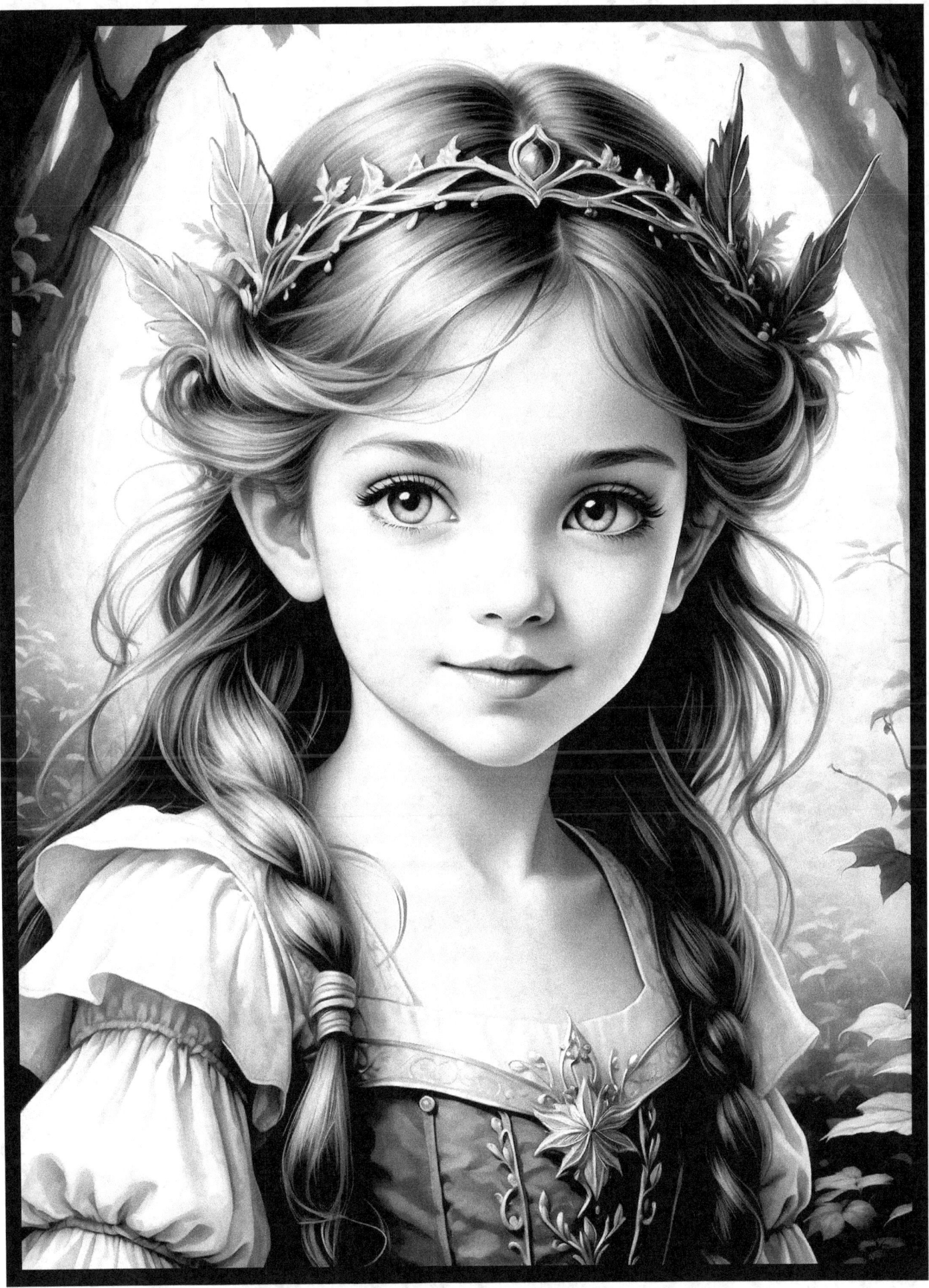

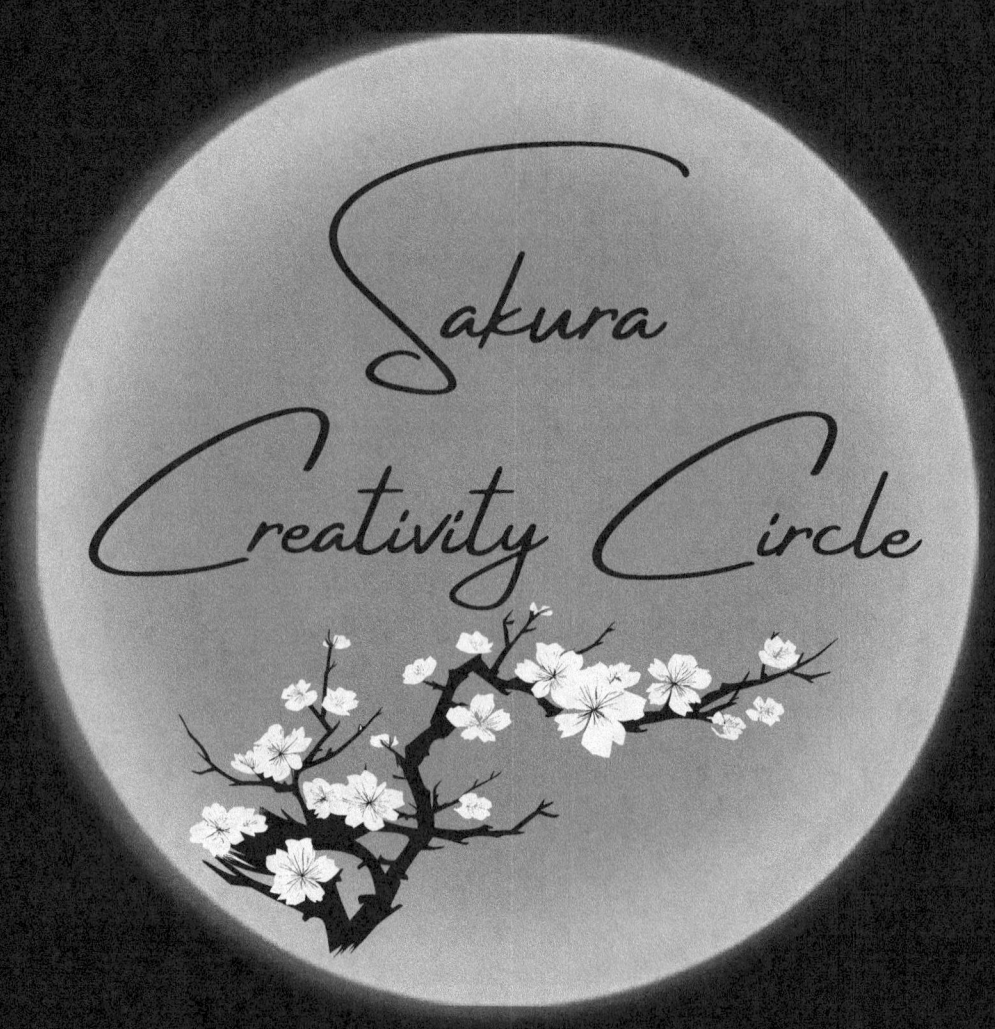

sakuracreativitycircle.com

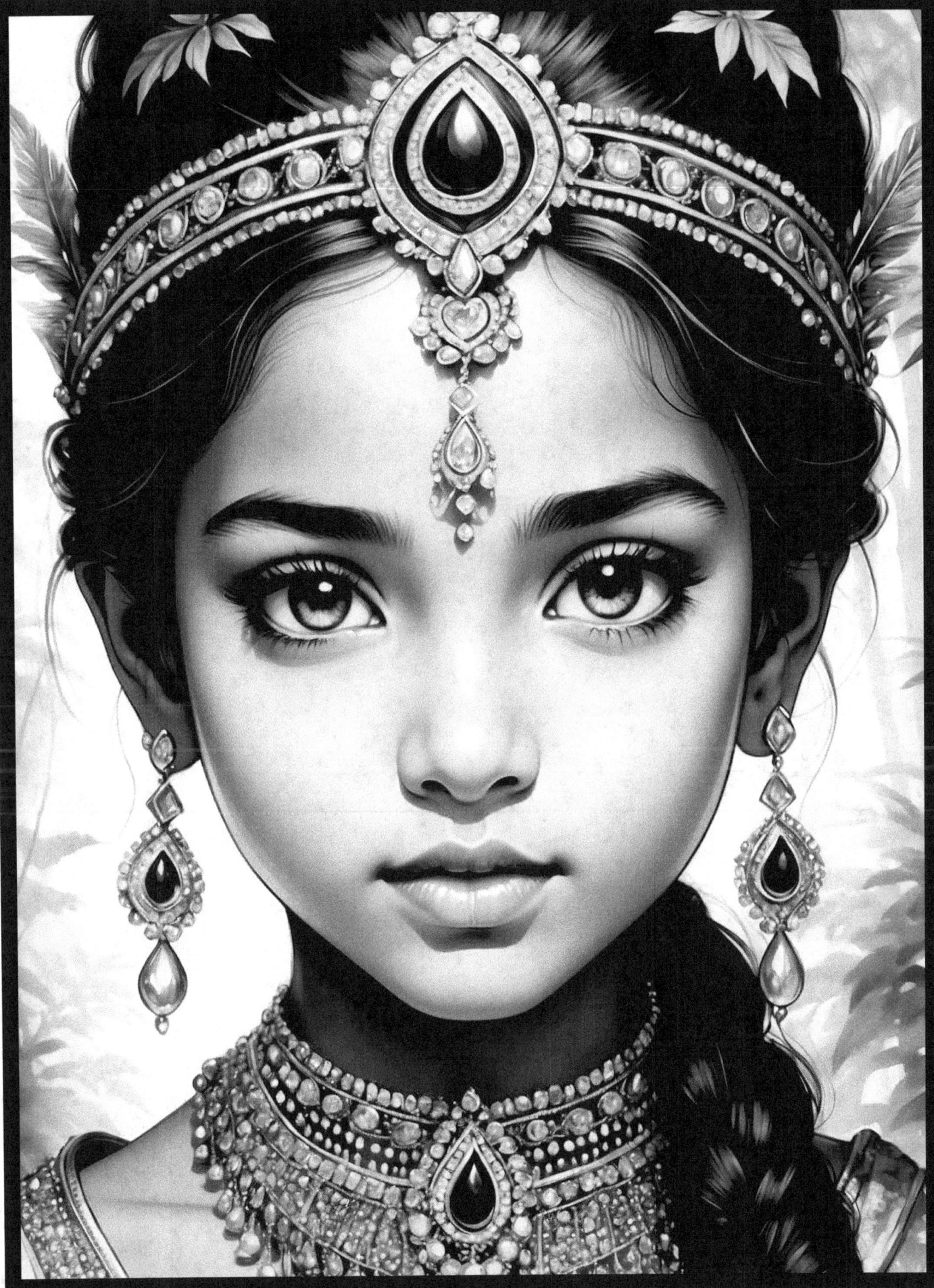

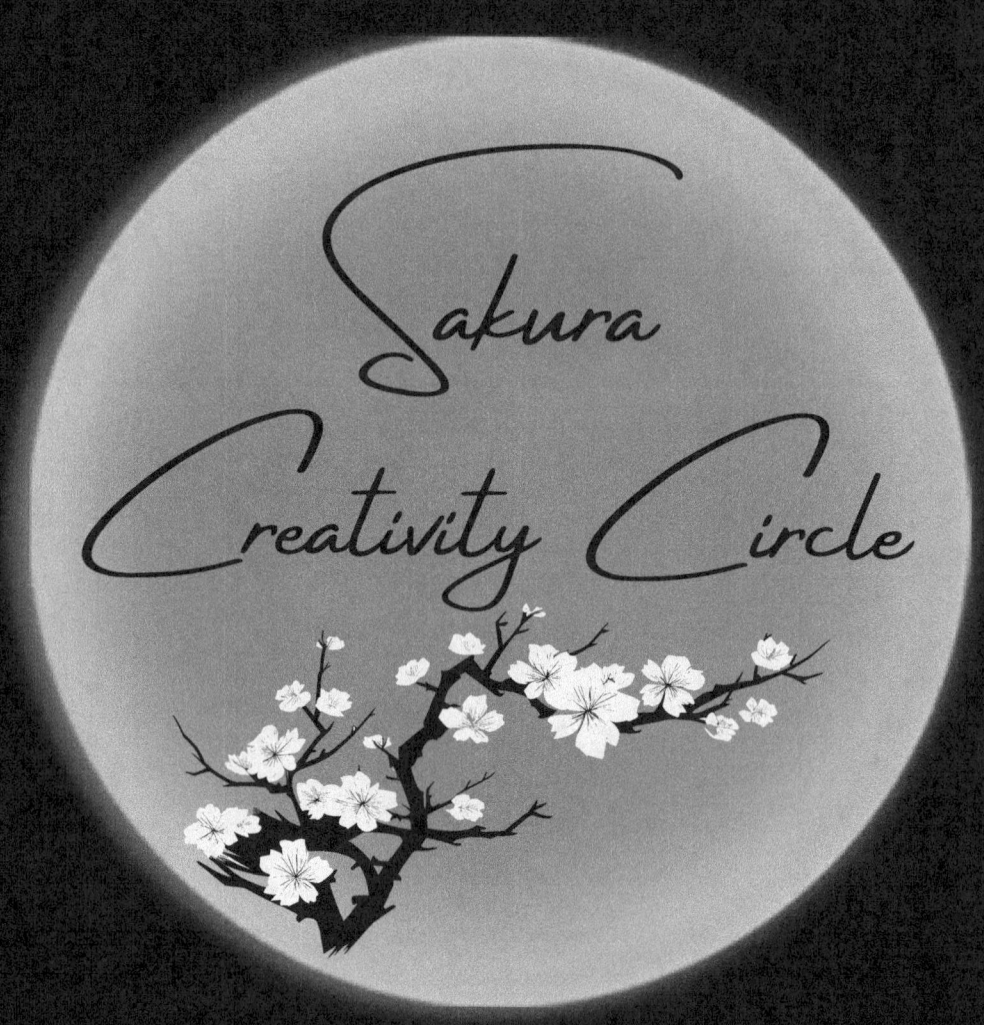

sakuracreativitycircle.com

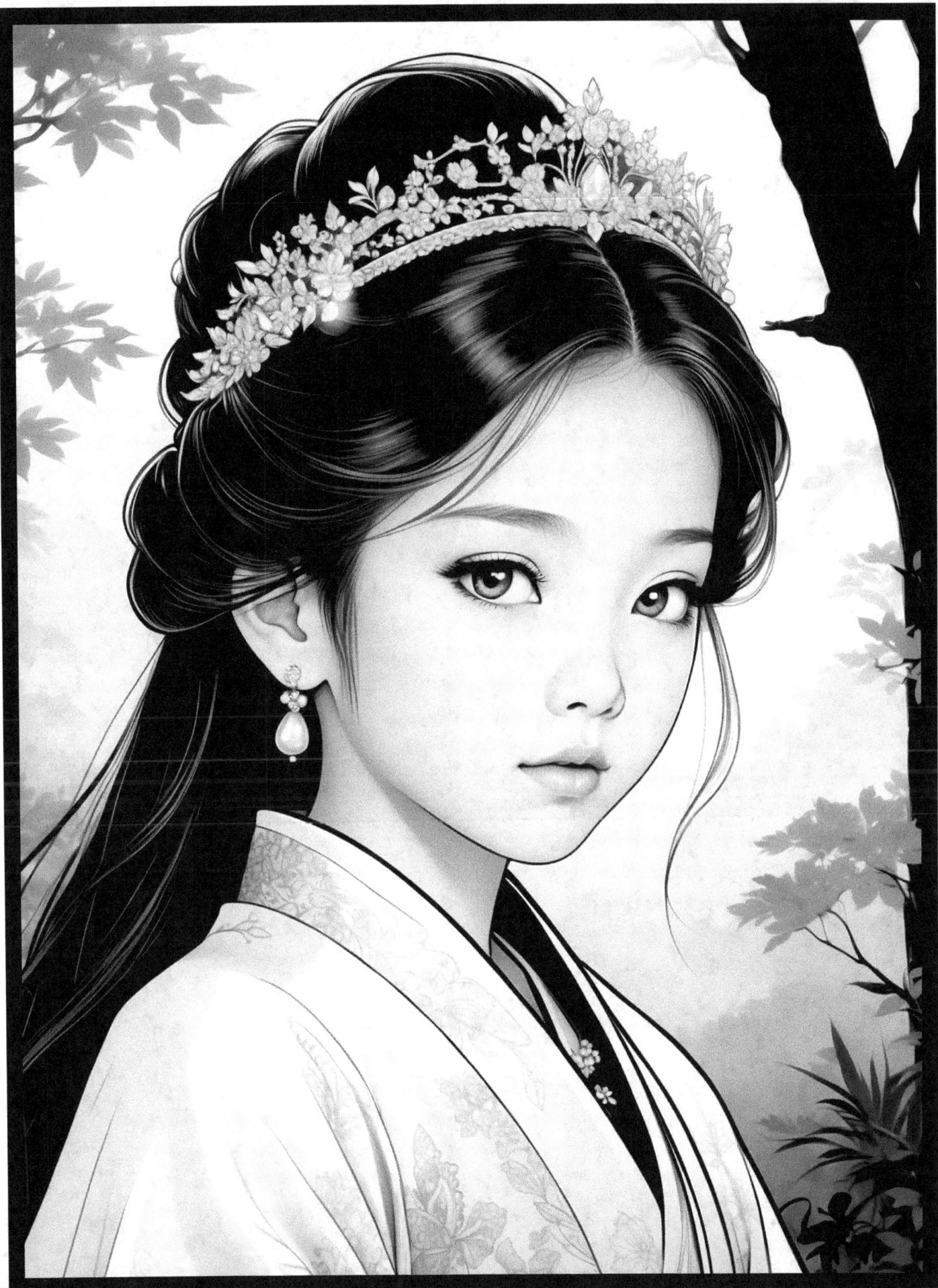

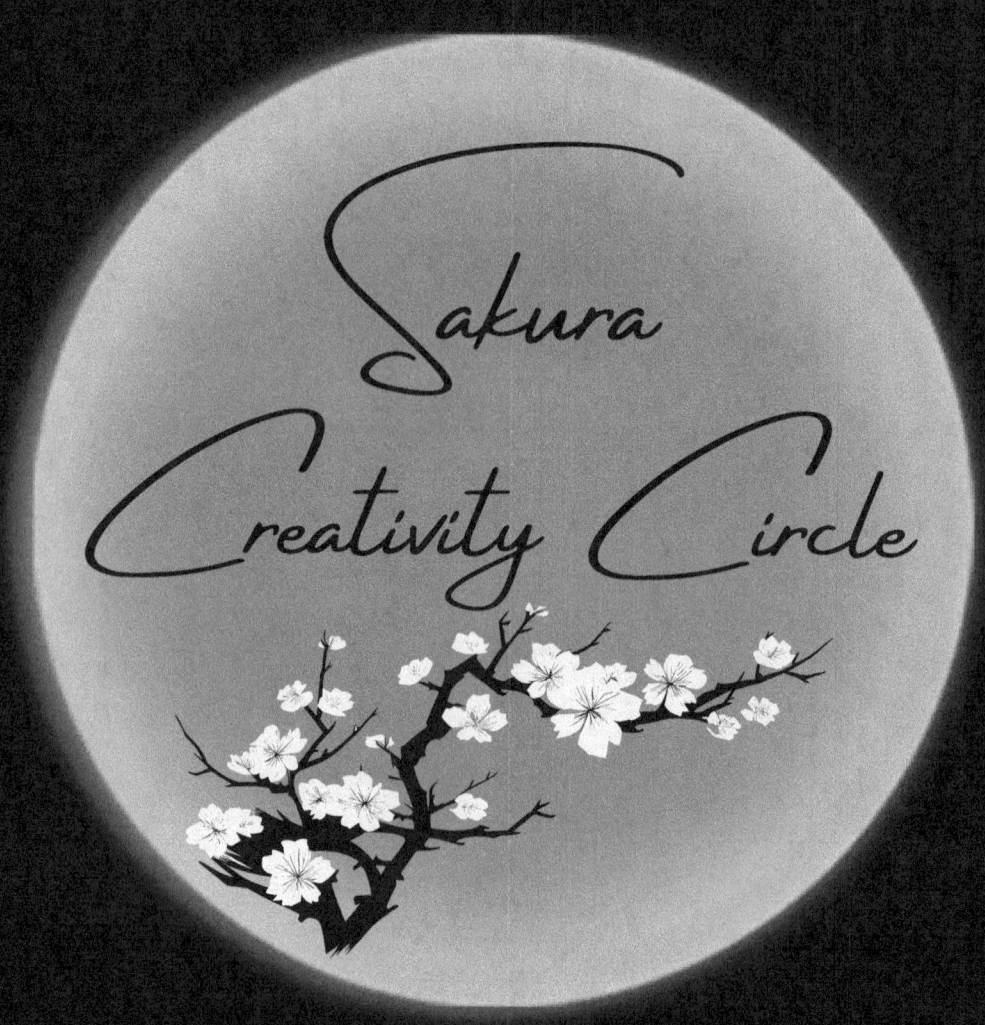

sakuracreativitycircle.com

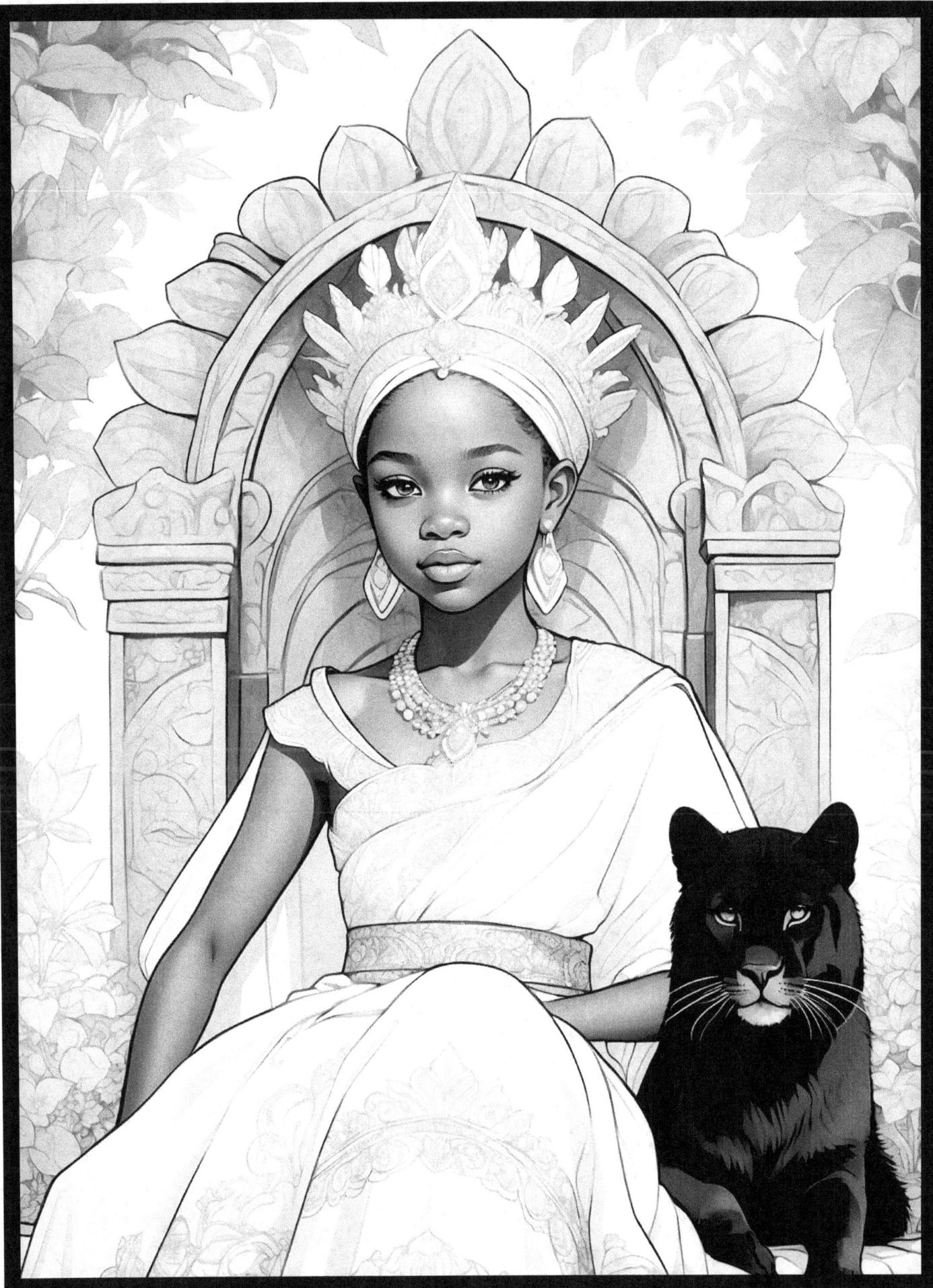

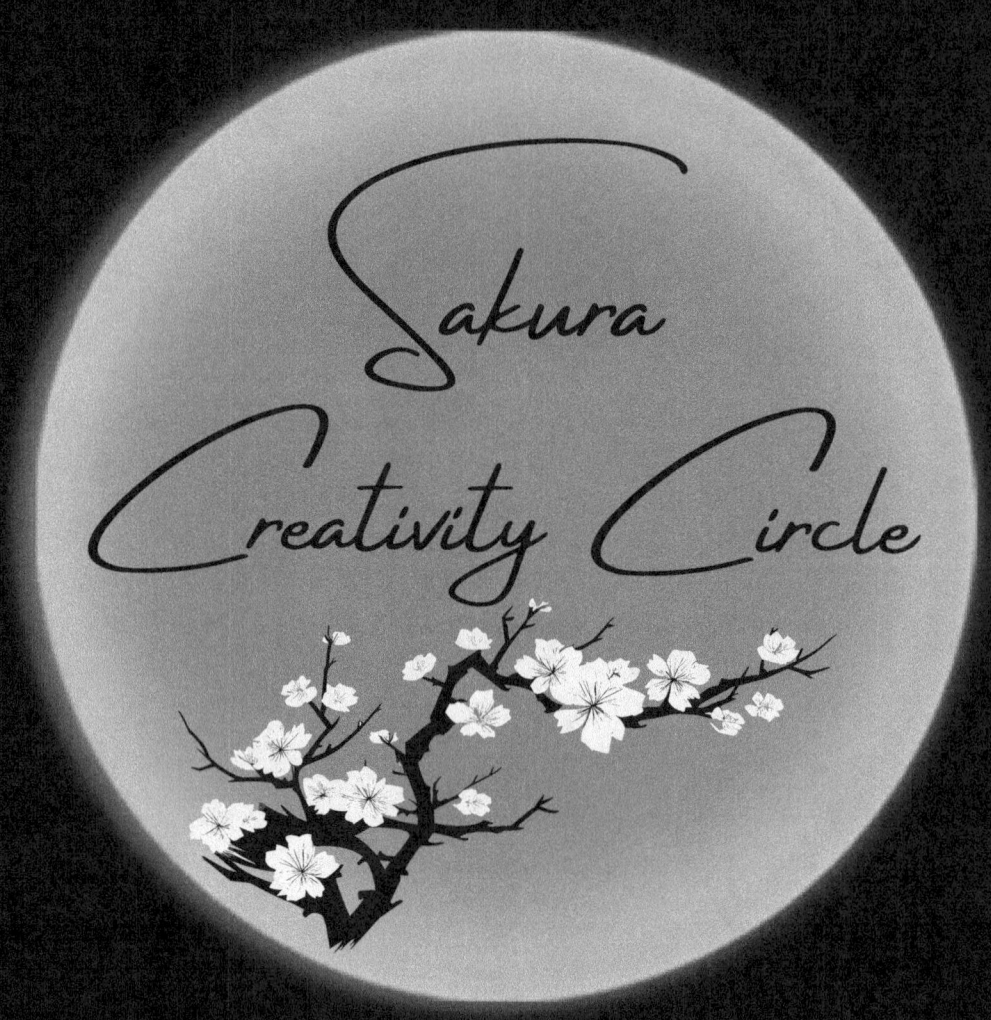

sakuracreativitycircle.com

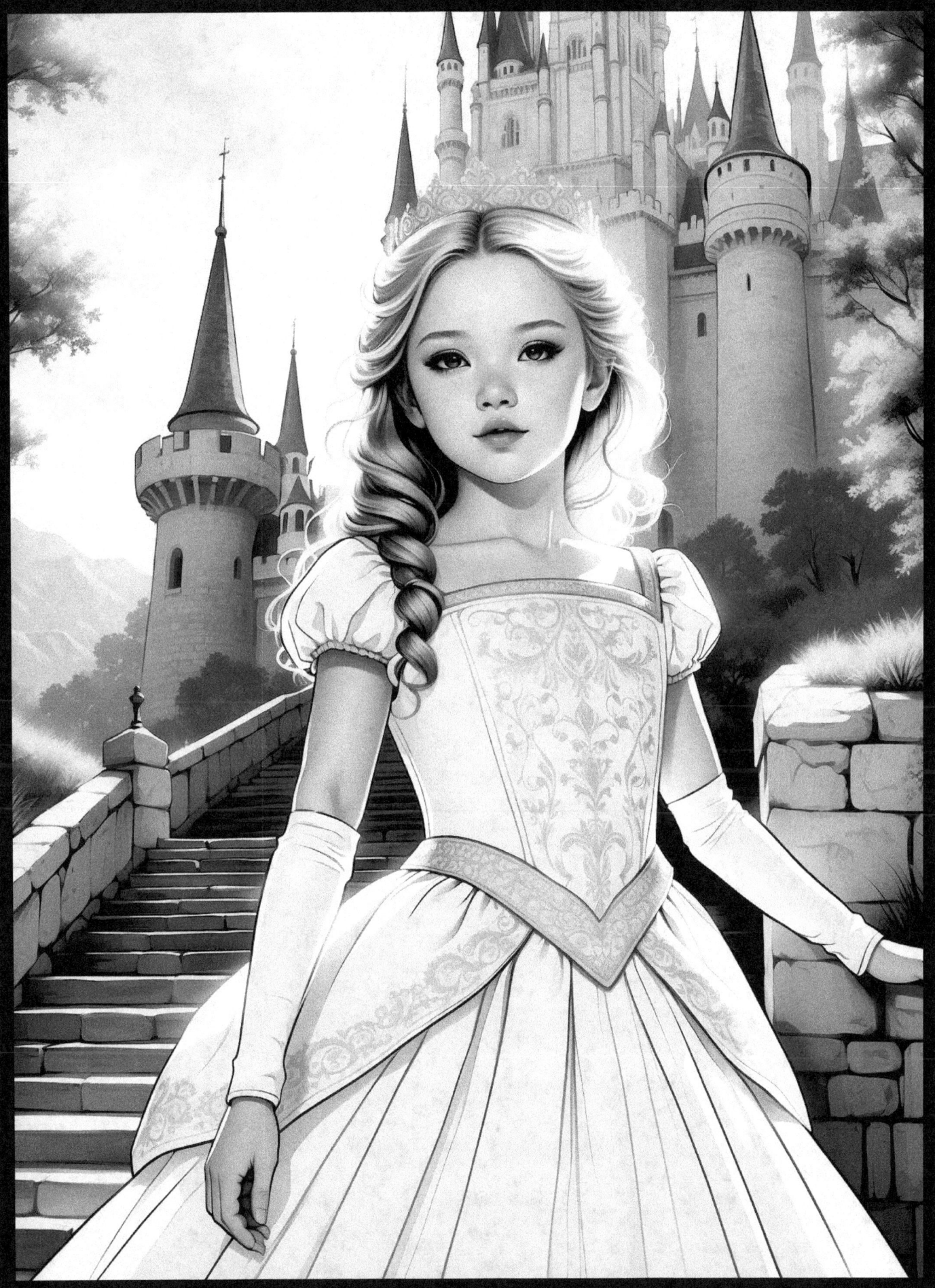

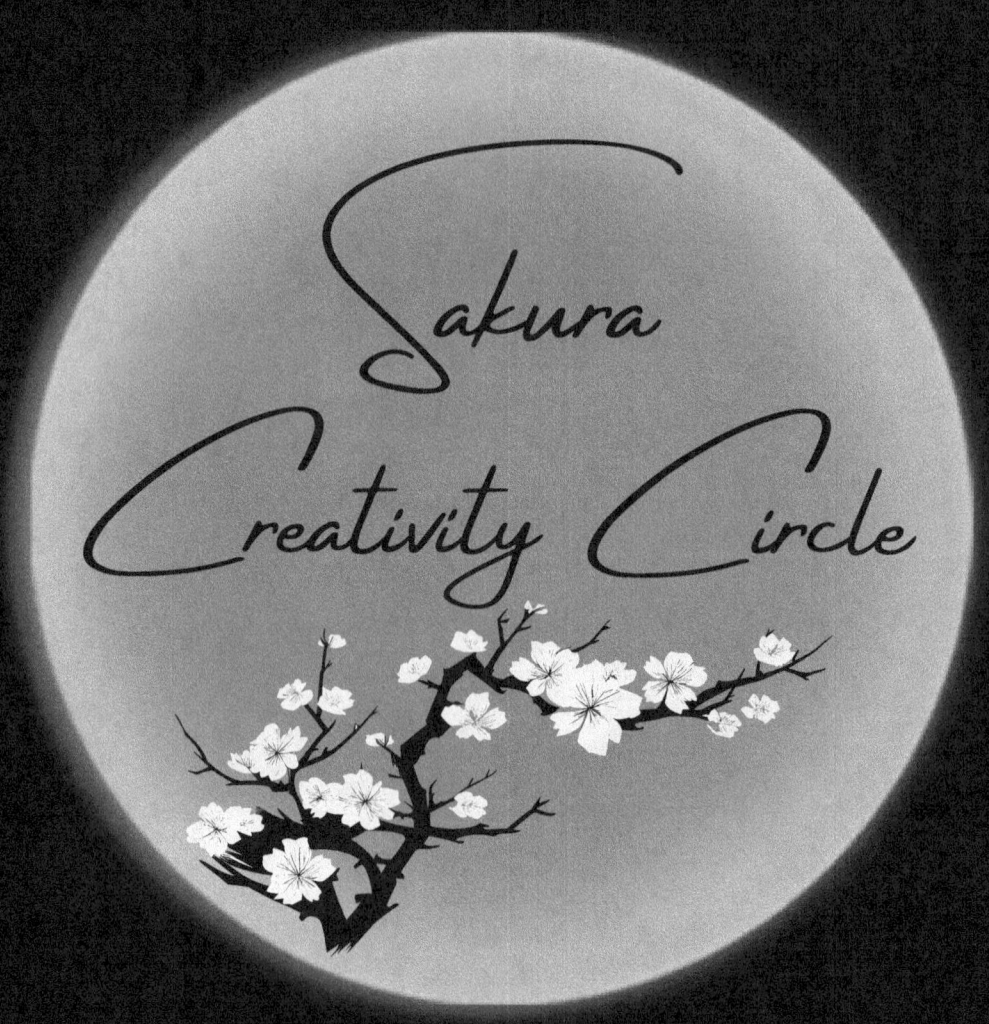

sakuracreativitycircle.com

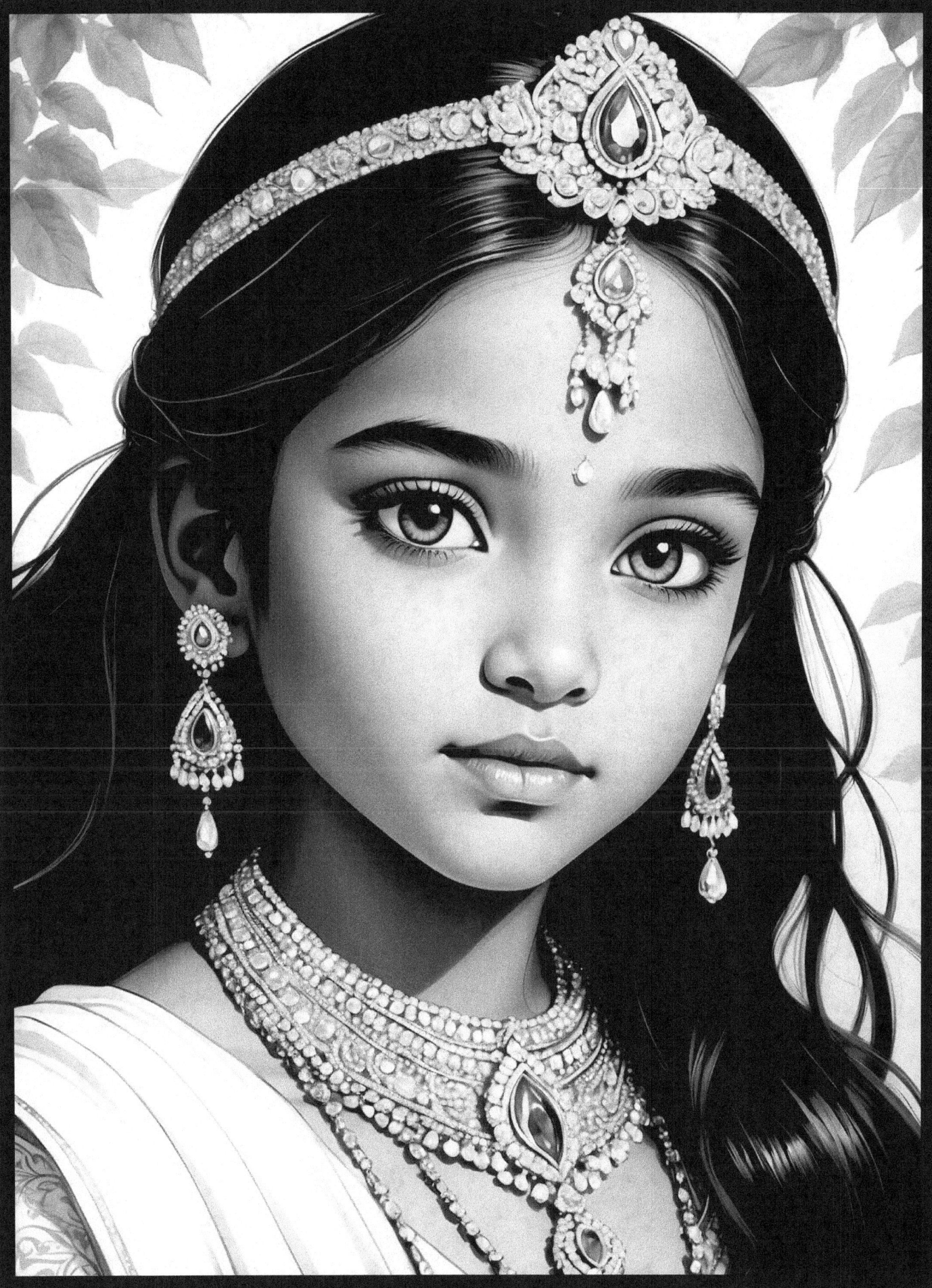

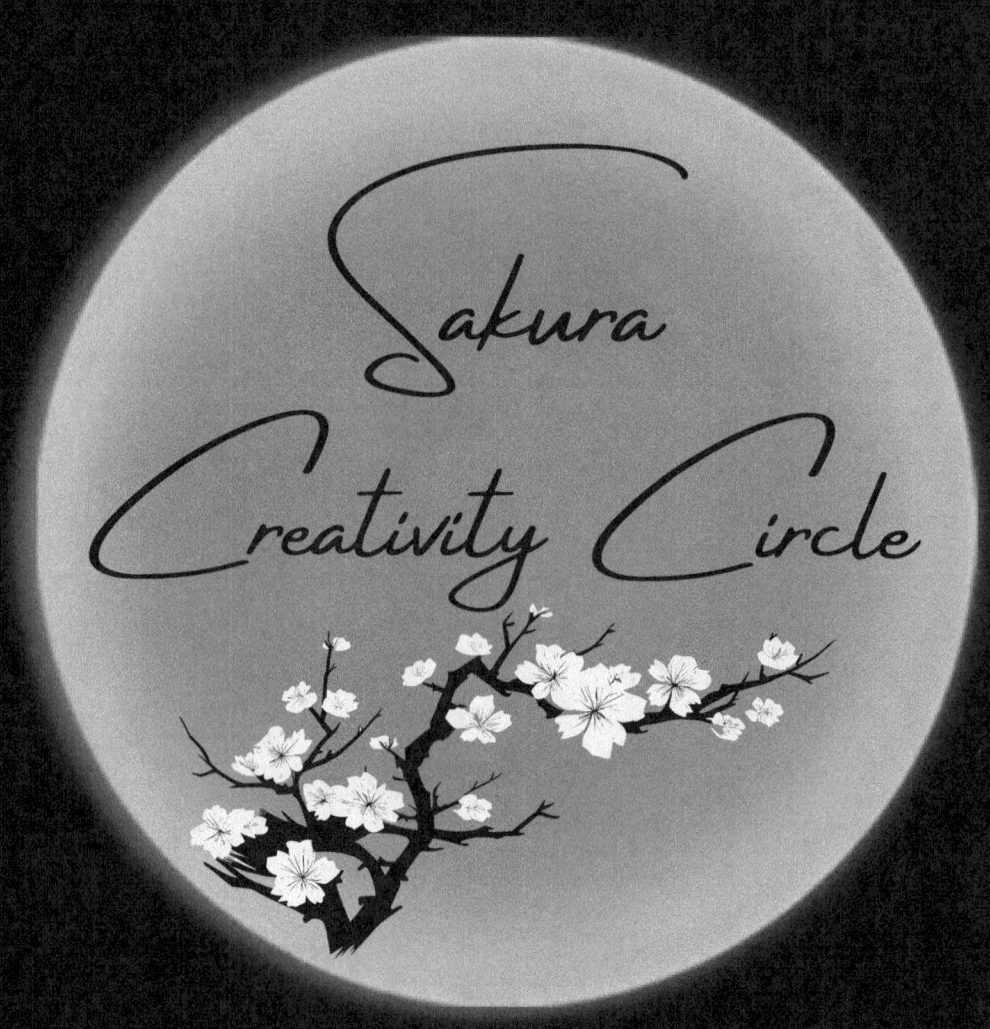

sakuracreativitycircle.com

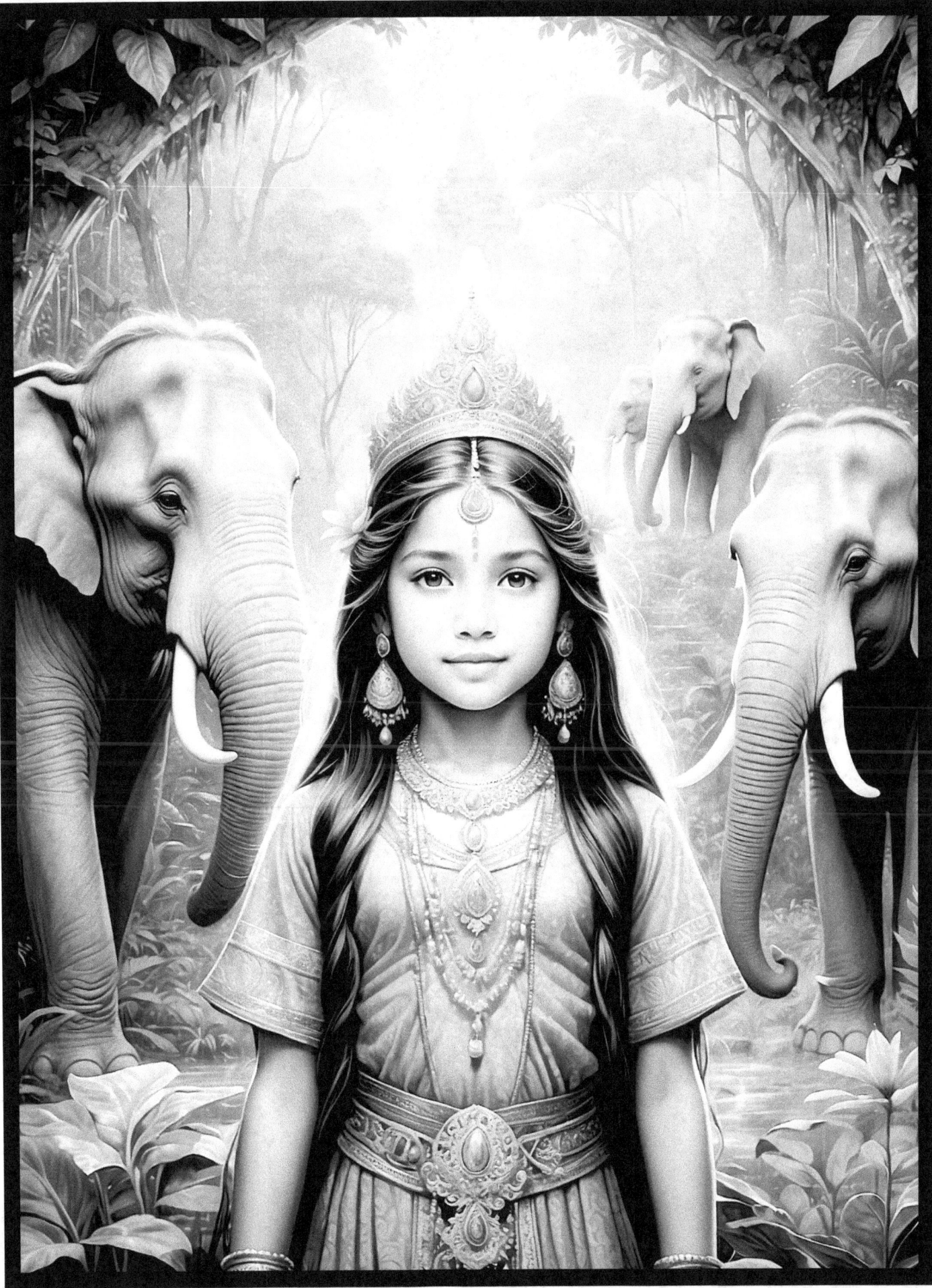

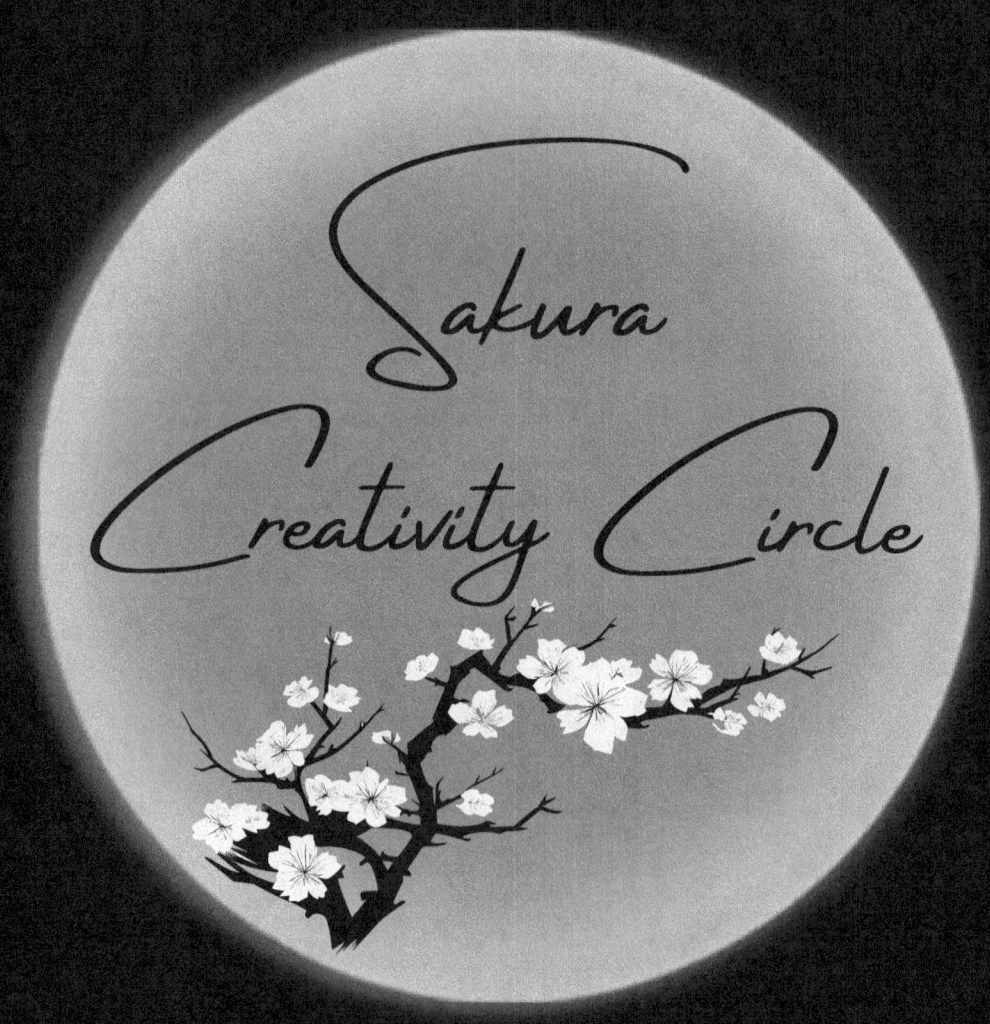

sakuracreativitycircle.com

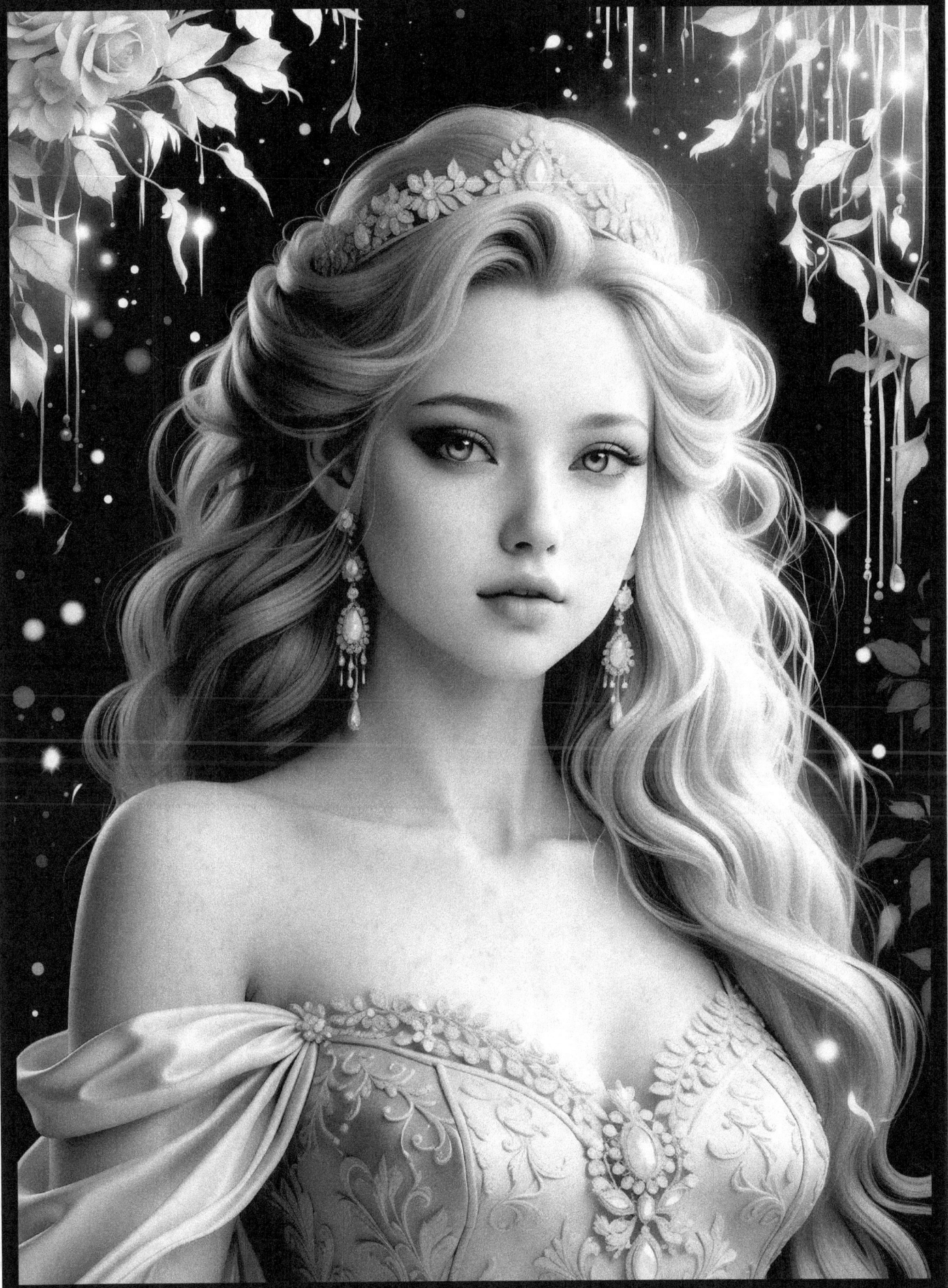

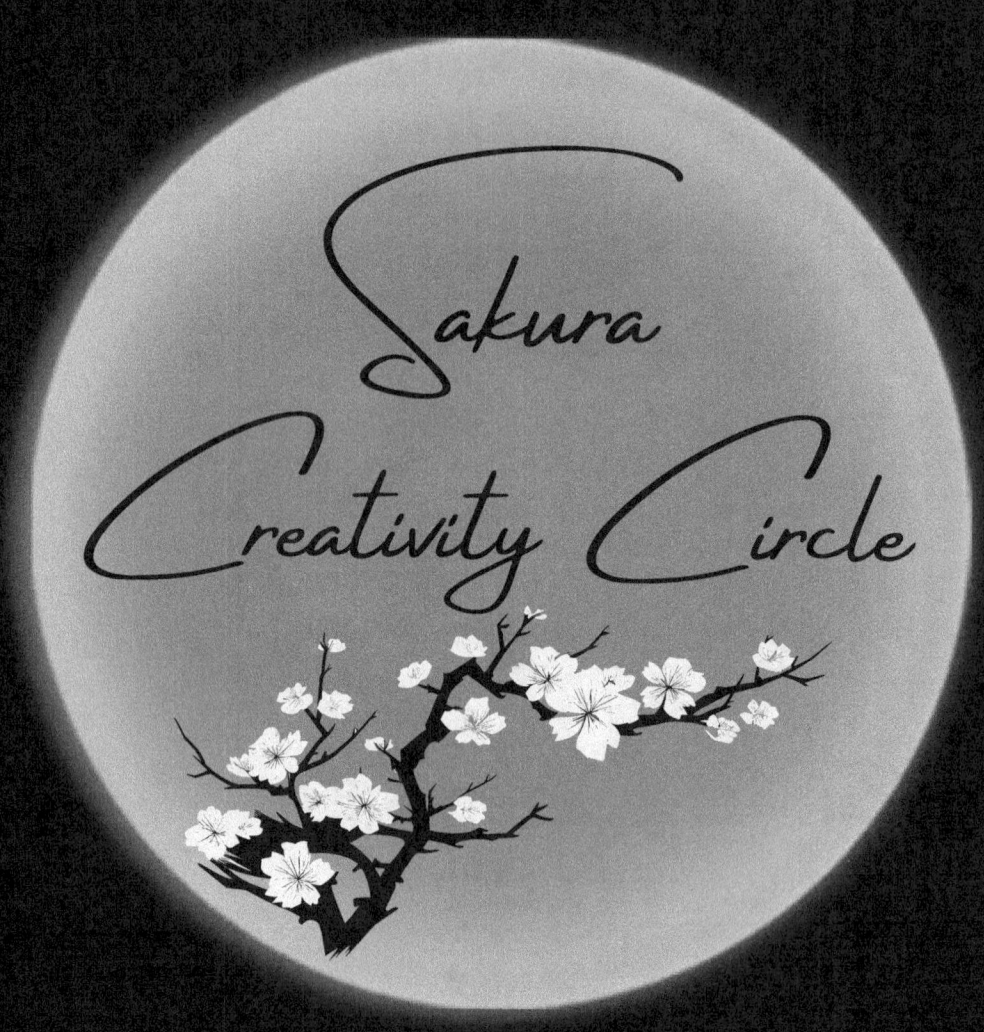

sakuracreativitycircle.com

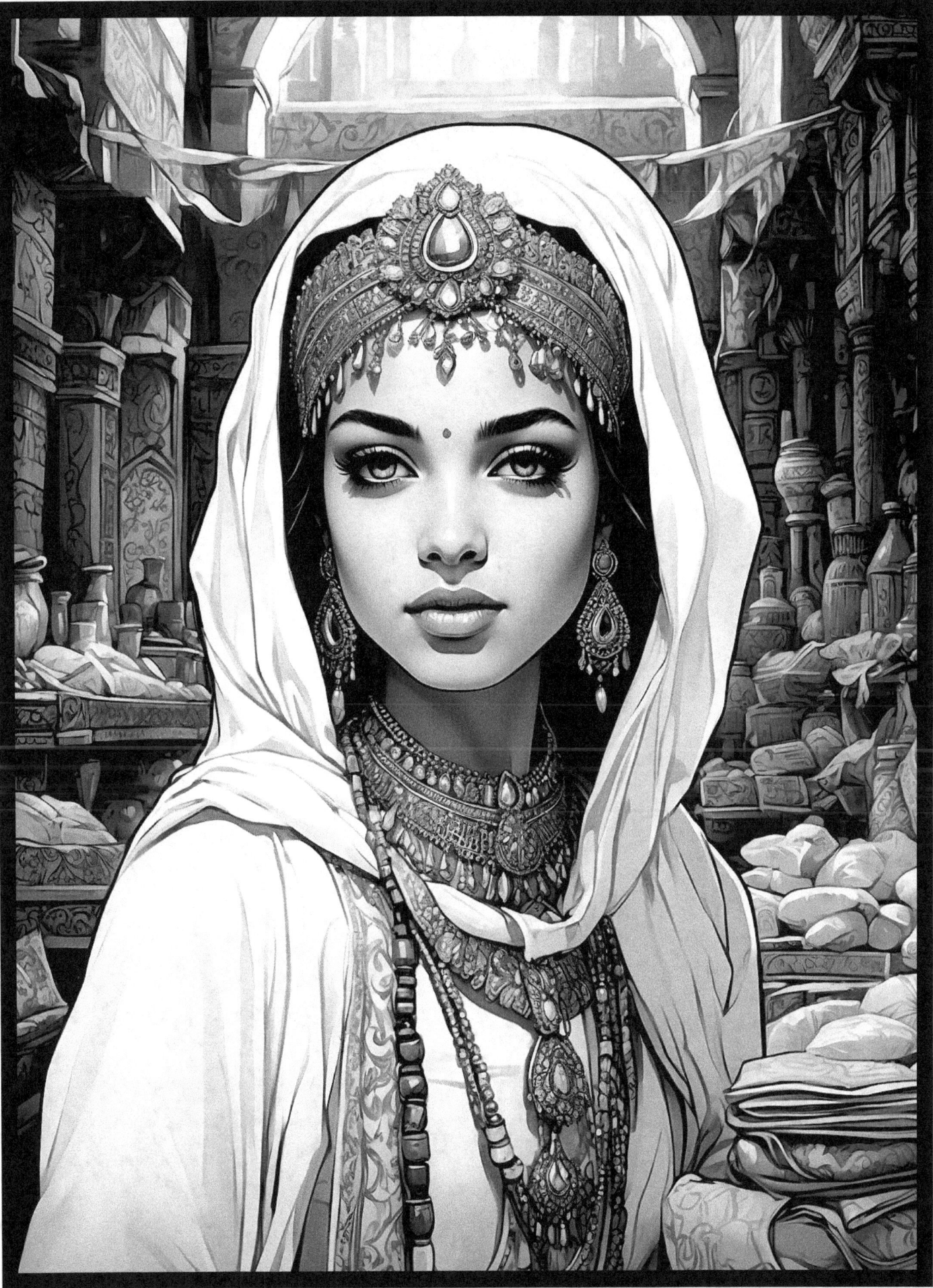

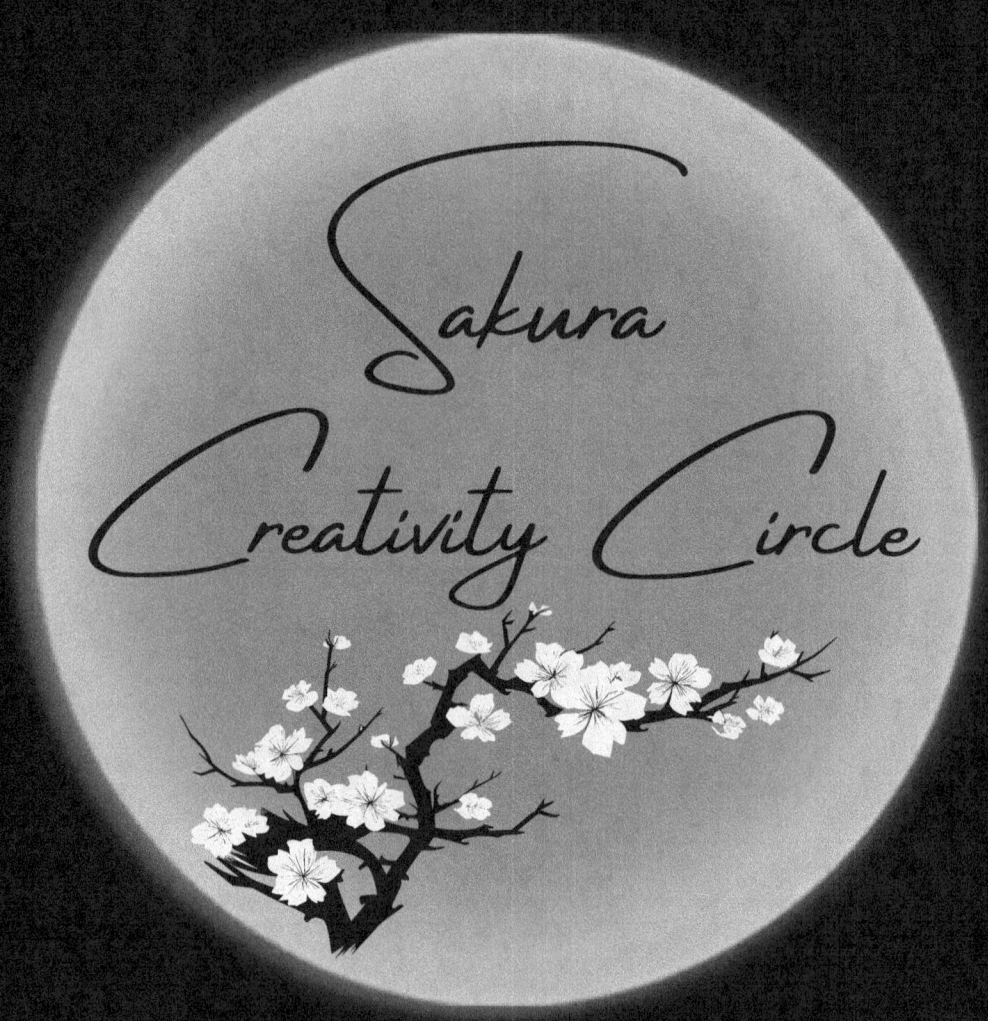

sakuracreativitycircle.com

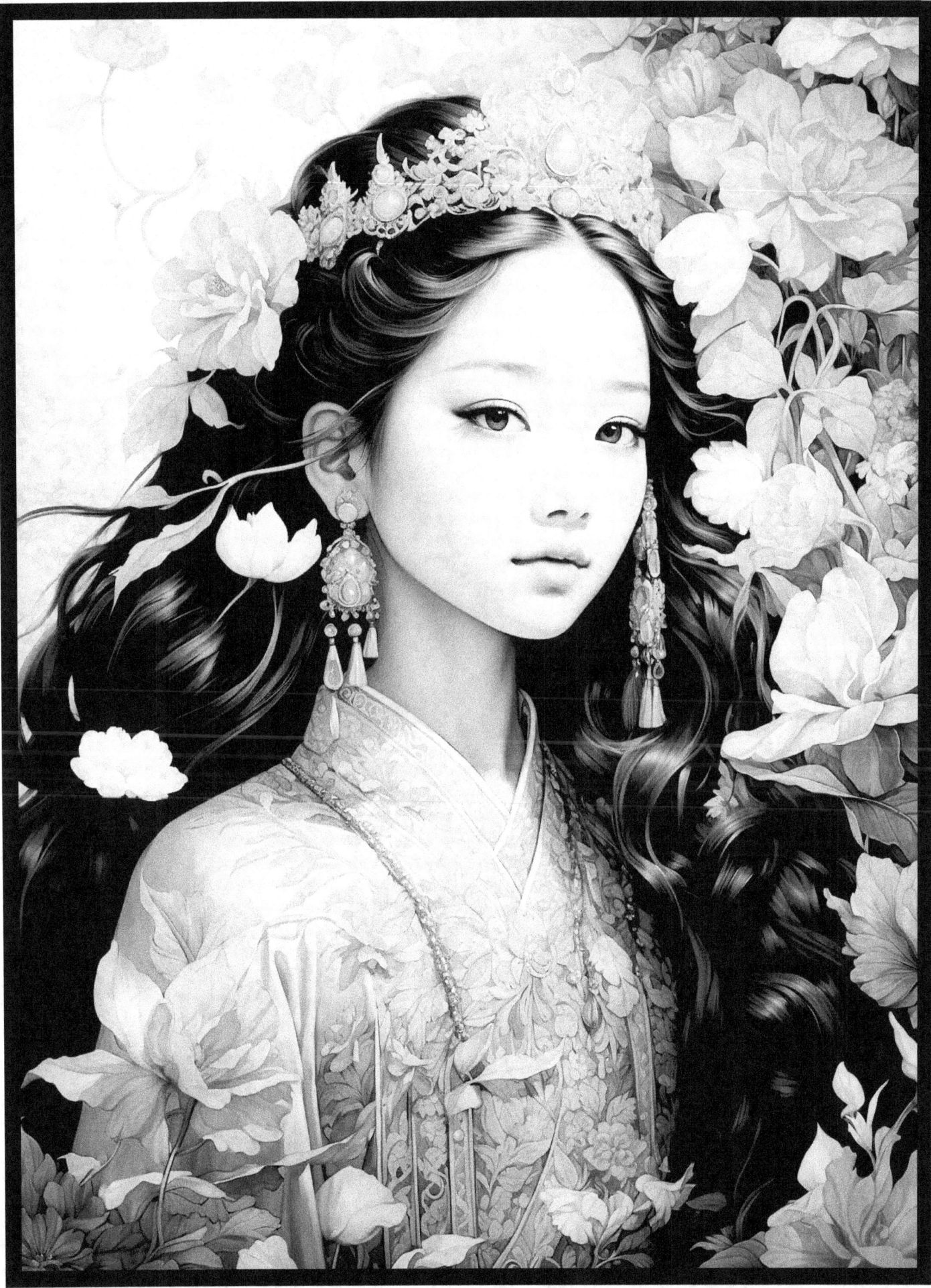

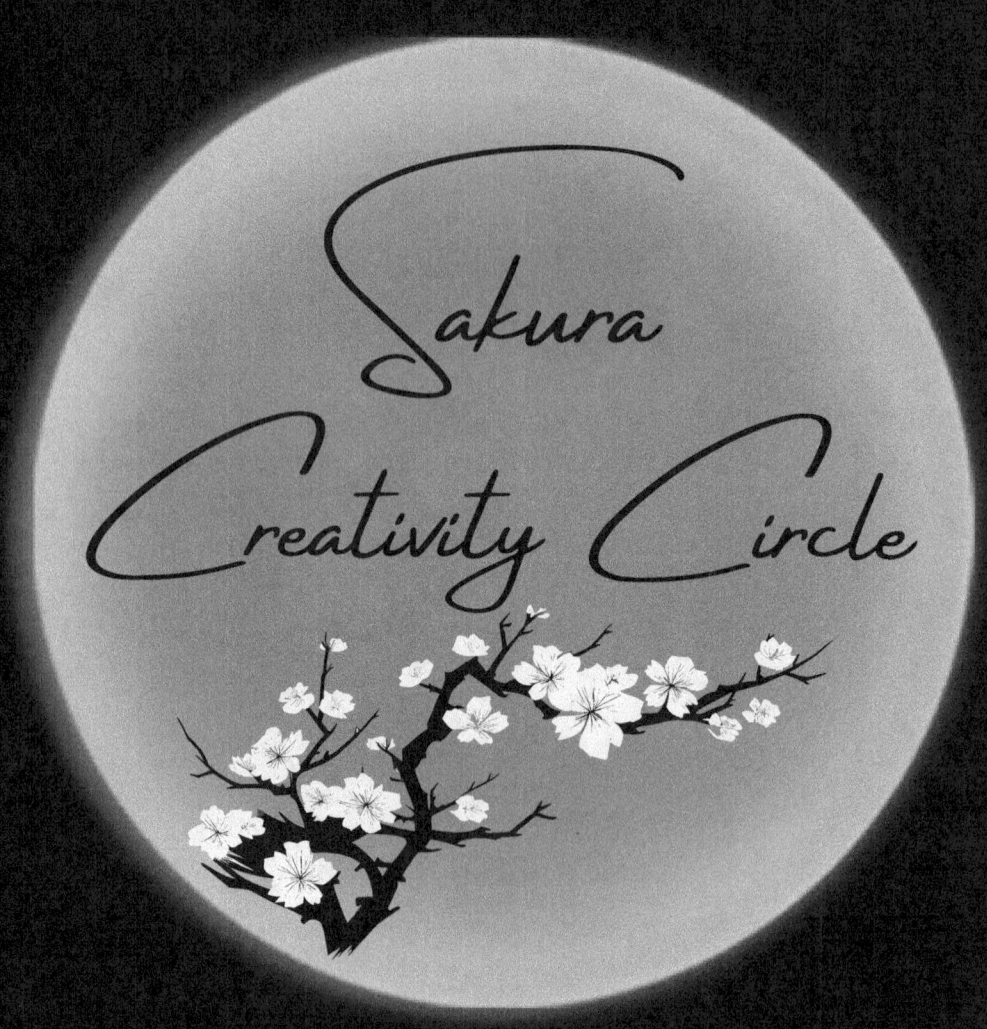

sakuracreativitycircle.com

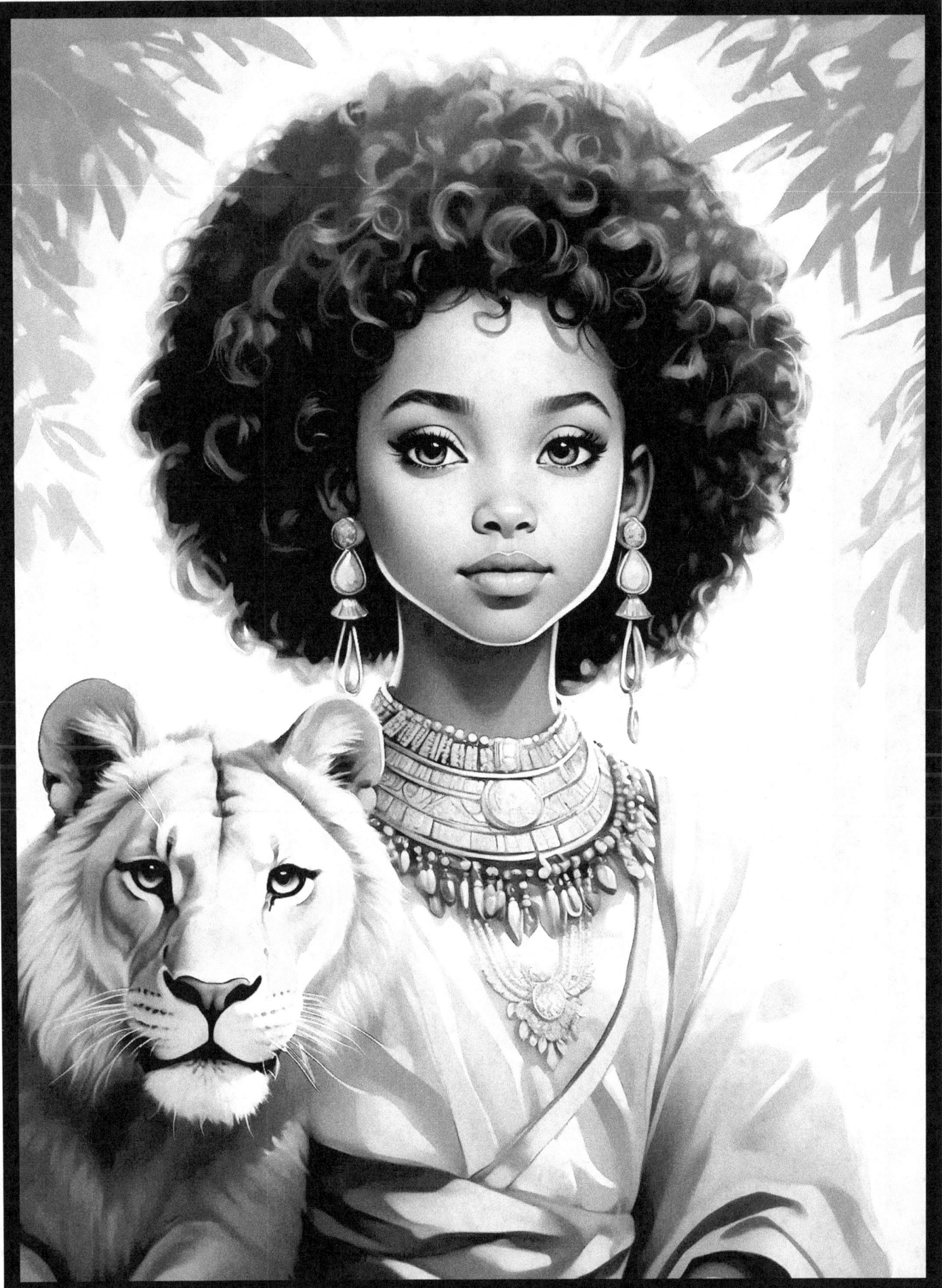

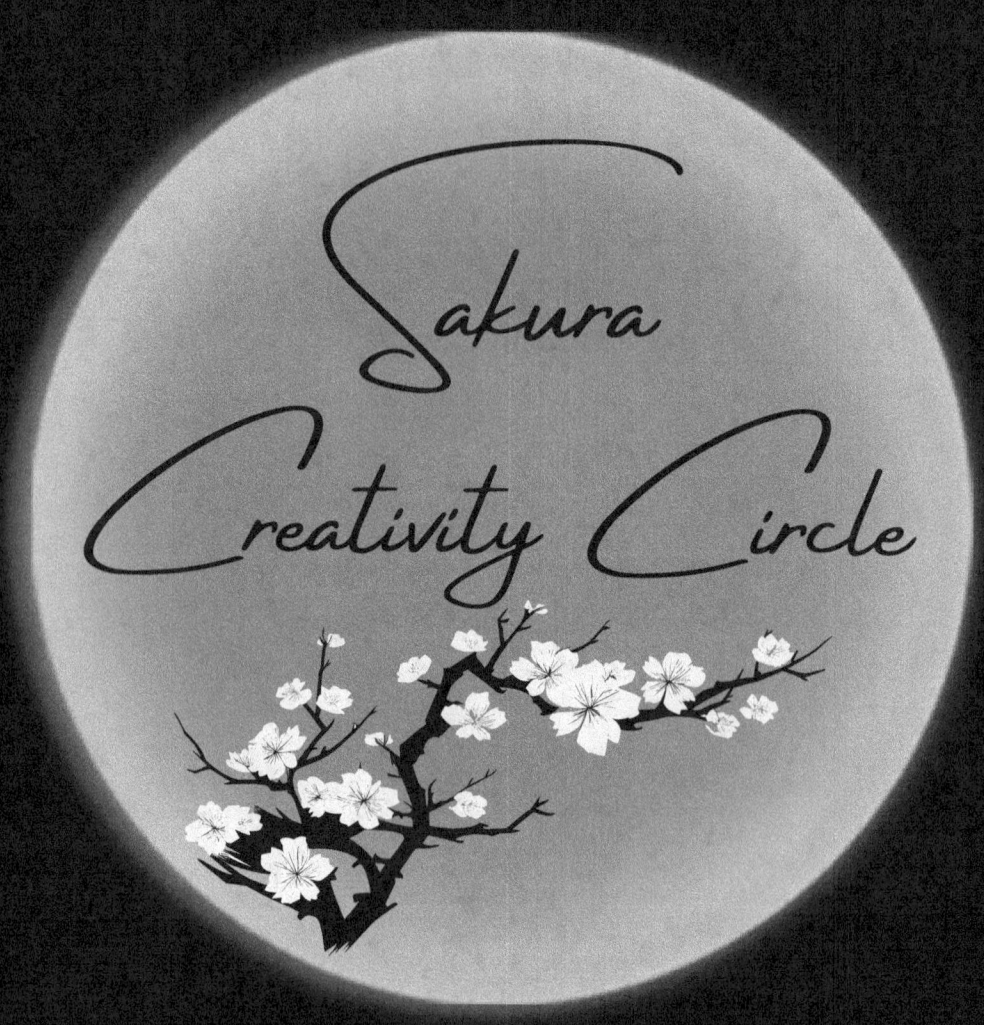

sakuracreativitycircle.com

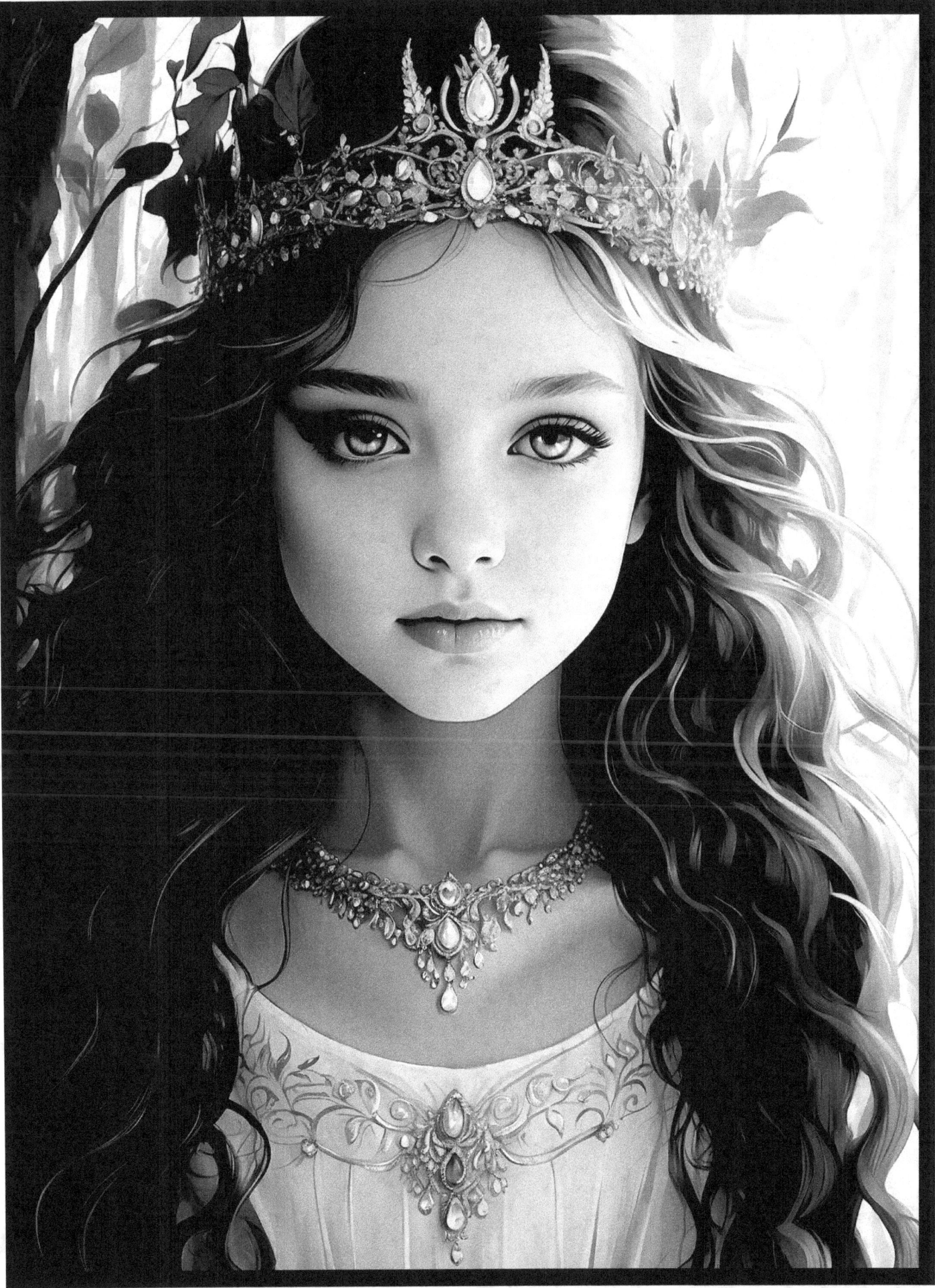

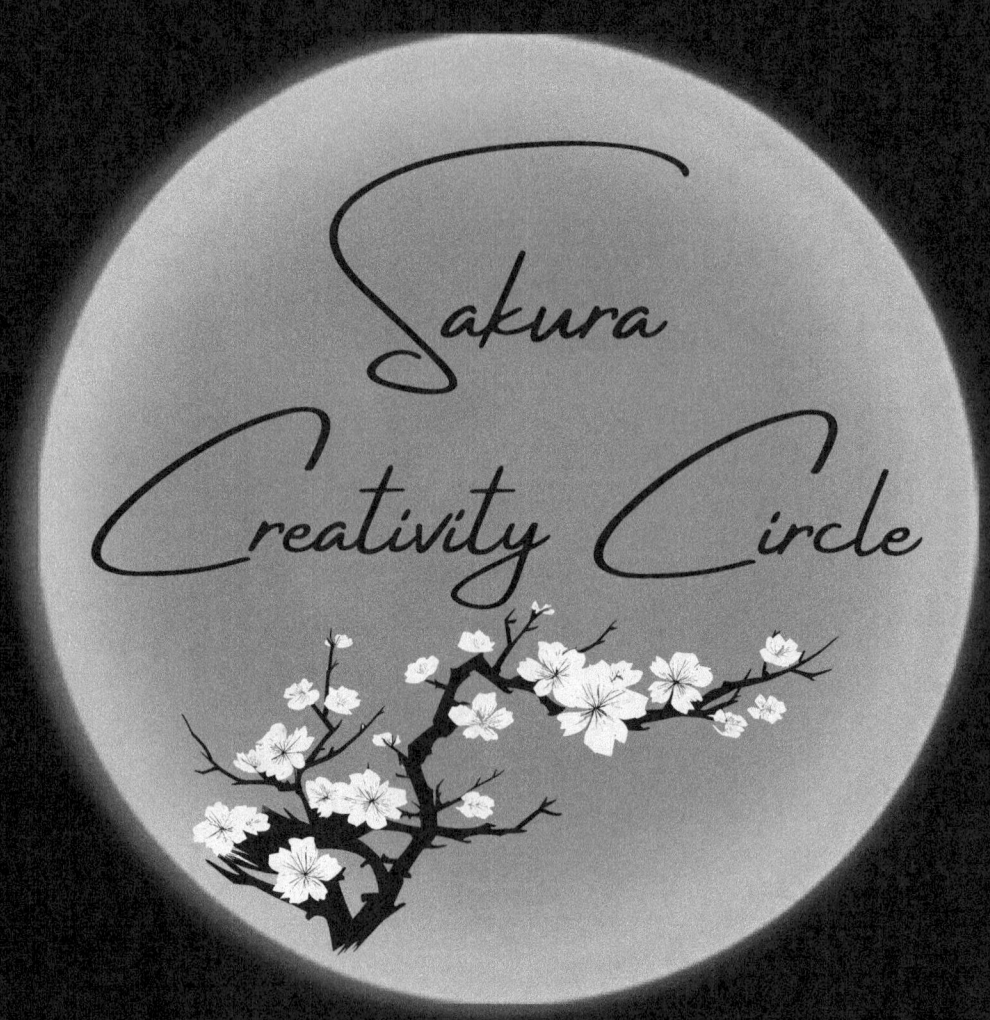

sakuracreativitycircle.com

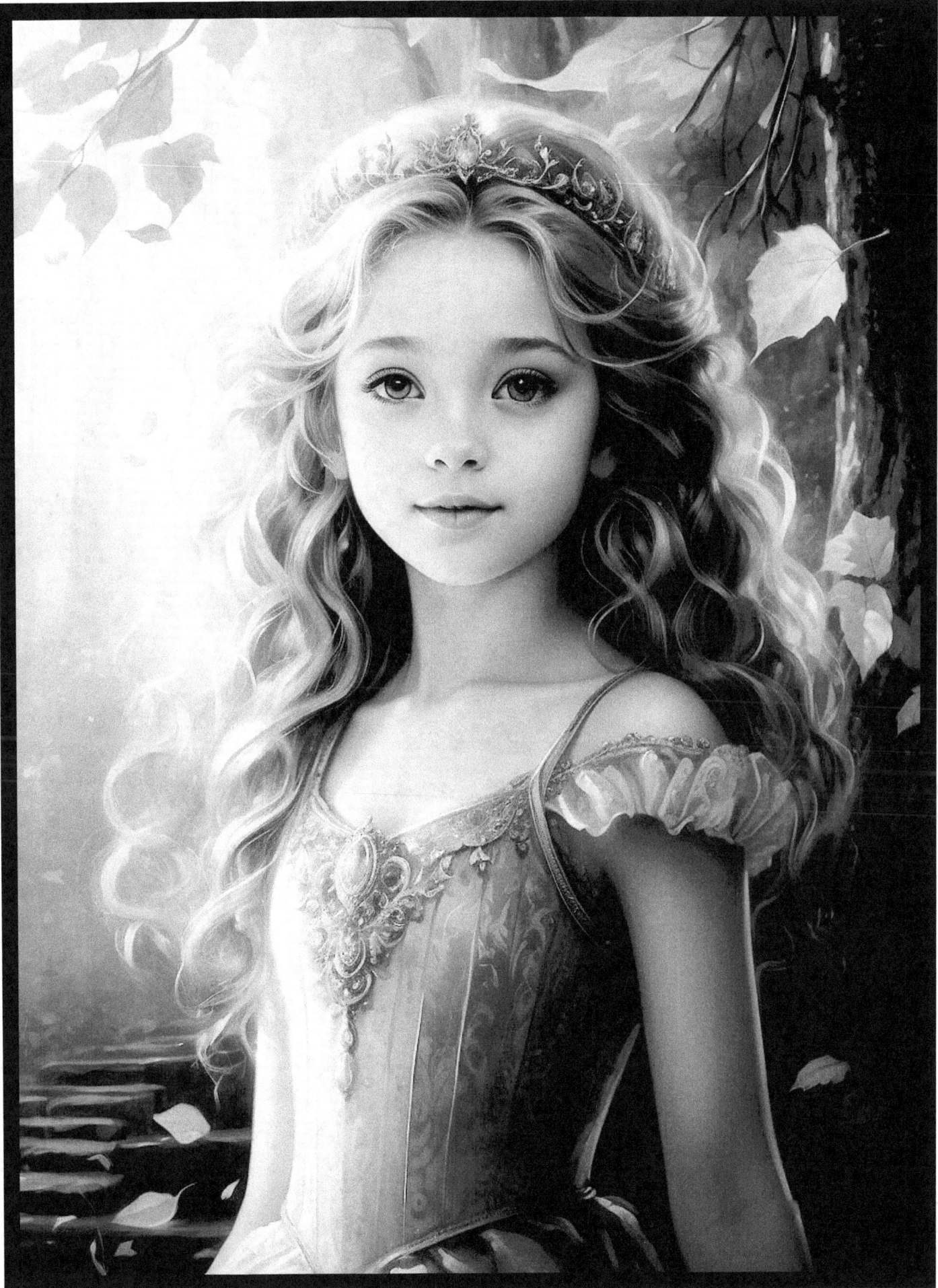

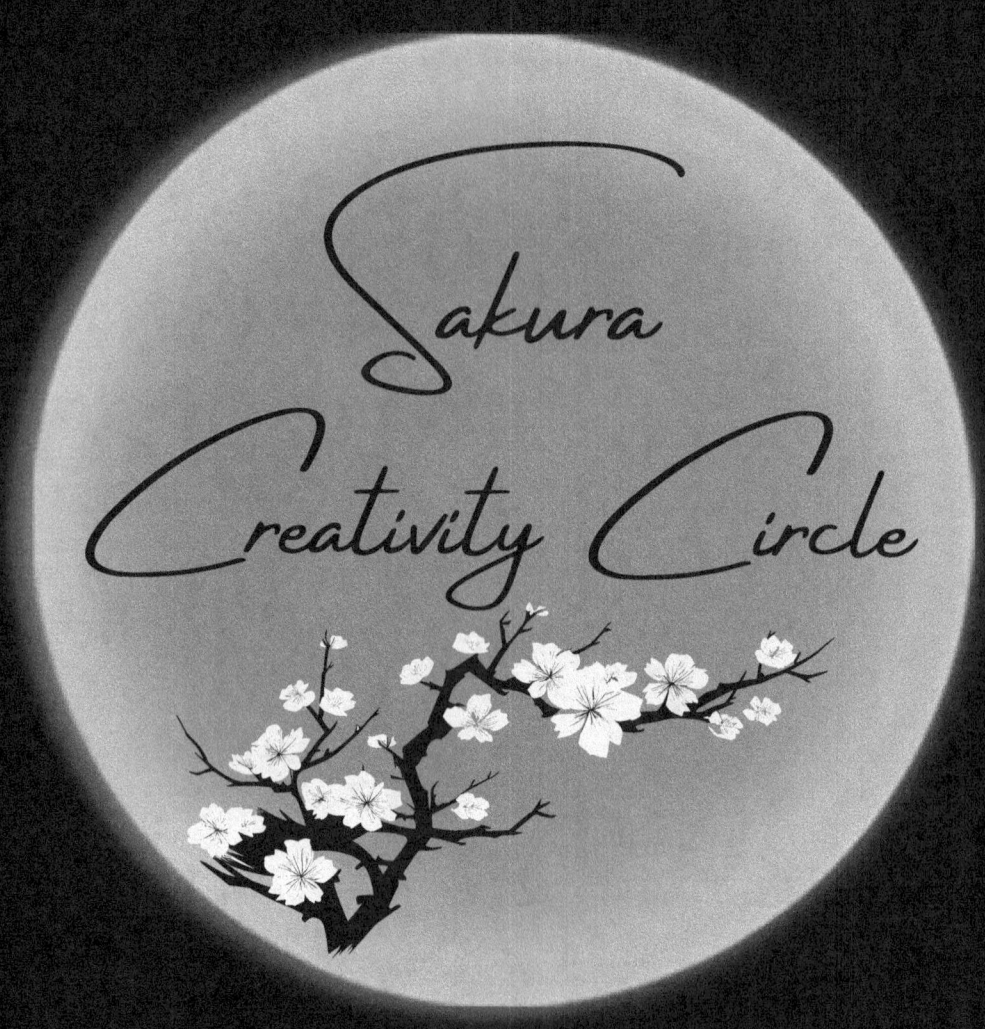

sakuracreativitycircle.com

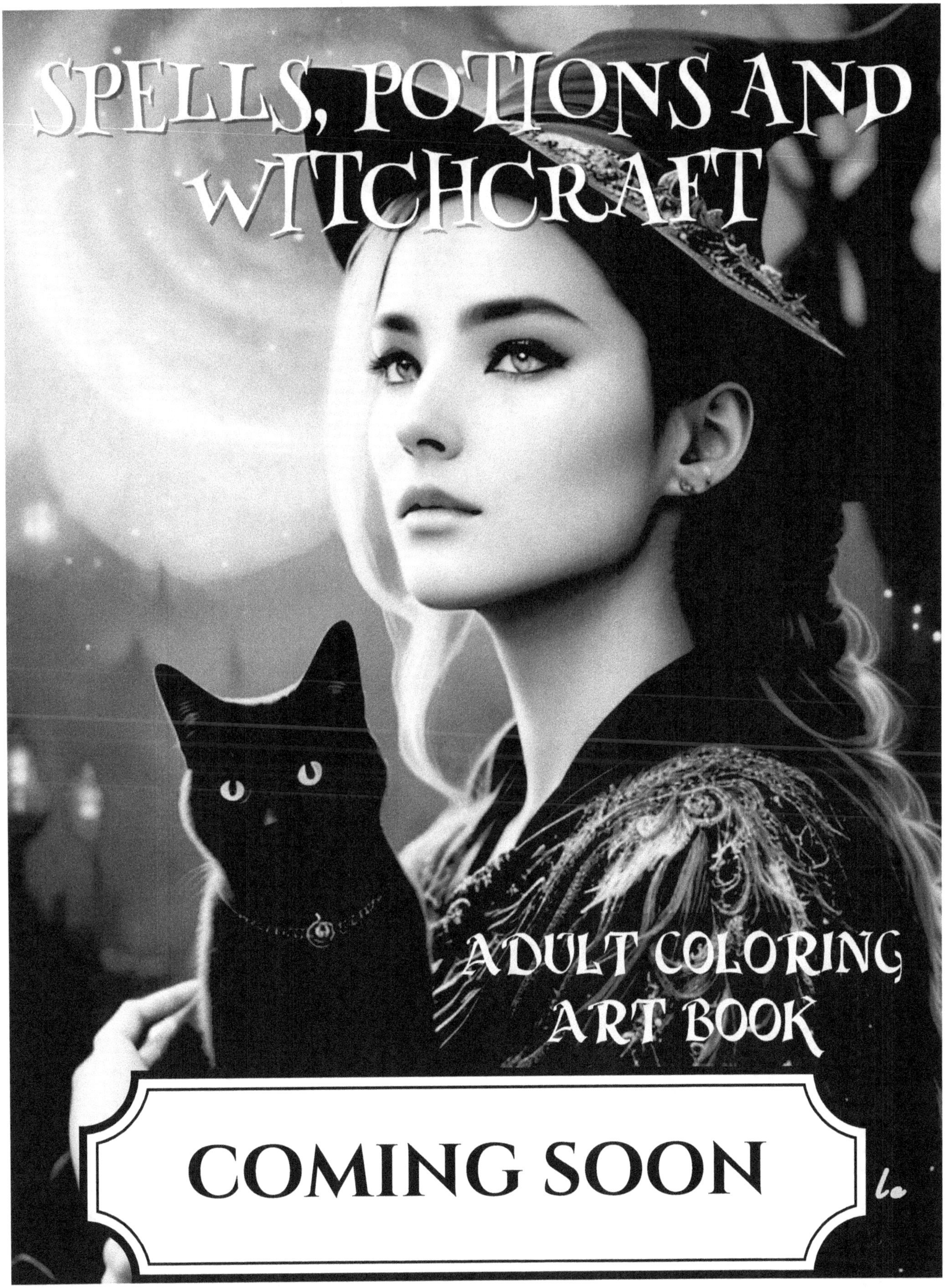
SPELLS, POTIONS AND WITCHCRAFT
ADULT COLORING ART BOOK
COMING SOON

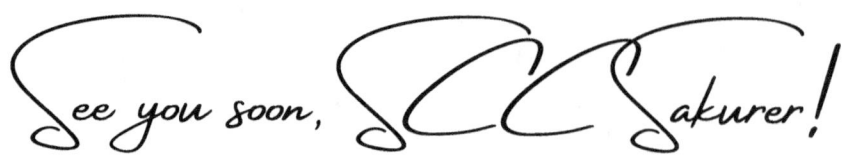

# See you soon, SCC Sakurer!

As we reach the final pages of "Fairy Tale Princess Coloring Book: Enchanted Realms," we hope you've found immense joy and inspiration in each stroke of color you've applied. As you close this book, reflect on the journey you've embarked upon — it's not merely a showcase of your coloring prowess, but a testament to your imaginative spirit, a beacon of inspiration that could lead others in the SCC community.

Whether you choose to share your creations and insights or keep them as your own cherished artworks, remember that in the world of SCC, every piece you create, every thought you share, adds to the vibrant tapestry of our community. Your voice is more than just commentary; it's a vital thread in the ever-evolving tapestry of creativity and innovation.

Thank you for joining us in this enchanting adventure. Your involvement is more than participation; it symbolizes your relentless pursuit of artistic excellence and innovation. We encourage you to proudly display your works and possibly inspire others to embark on their own creative journeys. At SCC, we're not just creating art; we're inspiring a community to push the boundaries of imagination.

See you soon with more creative adventures.

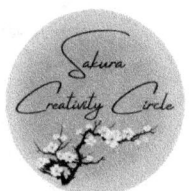

www.ingramcontent.com/pod-product-compliance
Lightning Source LLC
Chambersburg PA
CBHW082138290526
45794CB00008B/3079